Alienation and Beyond

Recent Indian Fiction

Alienation and Beyond

Recent Indian Fiction

Kamala Markandaya • Anita Desai

Arun Joshi • Kiran Desai

Chetan Bhagat • Aravind Adiga

Sarita Veerangana

prestigebooks
INTERNATIONAL PUBLISHING

Published by
Prestige Books
C 3/1, Janakpuri
New Delhi 110 058
Ph. 9818755529
email: prestigebooks@gmail.com
website: asiabookclub.com

Associate Office
60/29-45 Parramatta Road,
Concord, NSW 2137
Australia
ISBN: 81-7851-080-4

Printed at Chaman Offset Press, New Delhi 110 002

Contents

Further Explorations

With Gratitude and Love

For my Parents

Late Prof. K. B. Sahai

&

Mrs. Veena Sahai

Foreword

It gives me immense pleasure to write the Foreword to the book entitled *Alienation and Beyond: Recent Indian Fiction* written by Dr. Sarita Veerangana. The book is a high-end product of critical literary sensibility; it assorts a good number of essays on individual novels which are given an insightful, in-depth analysis and revealing, reader-friendly explications. Novel has always been a transcript of life. Consequently, modern Western novel has become almost an existential fable spelling out the contours of human reality. Indian English novel in its early stage, dealt with sylvan surroundings, peasant's problems, Independence struggle and such other allied subjects, but in its recent phase it has caught with the mainstream of global fiction. Alienation, angst, disinheritance, incommunication, loss of self and an incessant search for true identity are the common tenets of modern fiction as these form the matrix of experience in contemporary societies. In India also, particularly in the urban segment, life is no longer tranquil and wholesome. Alienation has become the *fin mot* of contemporary Indian life. Kamala Markandaya's novels explore the anguish of heterogeneity of culture, Anita Desai's novels foray the trauma of psychic incompatibility, Arun Joshi's fiction spells out the dimensions of existential dilemma and the novels of Kiran Desai, Aravind Adiga and Chetan Bhagat portray the socio economic and cultural turmoils resulting from industrialisation, globalisation and technological invasion prevailing in contemporary Indian life.

The book is fascinating not only for its powerful revealing but also by virtue of its immensely readable quality. Written in a lucid style, the critical essays exude the beauty of metaphoric and symbolic articulation. The book enriches the existing critical literature on Indian English novel. It will indeed be a valuable addition to the bookshelf of every sensible reader.

H. M. Prasad

(Dr. Hari Mohan Prasad)
Director, Academy of Foreign Languages and Cultural Co-operation
Former Head, Department of English and Dean, Faculty of Humanities
Magadh University, Bodh-Gaya.

Preface

Of late, Indian writing in English has gained momentum and has been recognized as an integral part of the literature of our country. Sanskrit was not the language of the Indians. It was the language of the Aryans who settled in India by ousting the Aryans. The Aryan settlement led to linguistic intercourse as a result of which a big body of literature in Sanskrit emerged. So was the case with Persian or Arabic language. They were not Indian languages. But now they have become part of Indian language. English language is also not the exclusive property of the westerners.

So far as Indian English fiction as a literary genre is concerned, it has unquestionably shown a capacity to accommodate a wide range of concerns. There are some distinguished figures in the field of fictional narrative, figures like Mulk Raj Anand, R.K. Narayan, Kamala Markandaya, Raja Rao, Bhabani Bhattacharya, Anita Desai, Manohar Malgonkar, Arun Joshi, Arundhati Roy, Khushwant Singh, Attia Husain and Gopinath Mohanty who have immensely contributed to the repertory of Indian English fiction to surprising success. In non-fiction, there are figures like Sri Aurobindo, Jawaharlal Nehru, N.C. Chaudhuri, Coomaraswamy, P. Lal and Nissim Ezekiel.

Contemporary Indian English fiction is multi-dimensional. It has spread in several directions dealing with racial prejudices, economic disparity and tribal violence to domestic and marital problems. But one of the most prominent and conspicuous traits of the Indian English fiction of our time is the theme of alienation, the subject I have chosen for this study. Alienation means a sense of withdrawal, rootlessness, isolation, loneliness whether it is caused by a temperamental incompatibility between the married couple or by cultural interaction, economic or linguistic factors or value systems telling upon the psyche of the characters.

It is a matter of common experience that in the world we live in, things have fallen apart. We hardly look beyond our nose. This change in mentality has much to do with our normal living. The husband and the wife live under the same roof. But the lack of understanding between them plunges the wife into an abyss of unmitigated trauma. The other side of the coin is no less dubious. The husband is so much self-obsessed that he never feels the agony of his counterpart. The wife feels completely alienated. Cultural encounter is also responsible for alienation. An Indian living in a foreign country hardly feels at home there and despite his best attempts to identify himself with the foreigners he never gets mixed up in the foreign soil as a result where of he feels completely alienated there and even after he comes back to his own country his habits do not allow him to remain an Indian. Cultural interaction and dislocation precipitate into a disastrous situation and the worst victim is the man who leaving behind his own native land, moves on to a foreign land inebriated by its glitter and glamour. The whole problem of alienation is existential, born of clash of culture.

There are many dimensions of alienation, the sociological or cultural, psychological and existential. Two of Markandaya's novels, *The Coffer Dams* and *The Nowhere Man* have been selected to show how cultural interaction dwindles into deculturation when one culture begins to efface another. In the former, the westerners are shown in the tribal region of India caught between technology and primitive faith and in the latter the representative Indian is portrayed in the backdrop of London oscillating between acceptance and condemnation.

Anita Desai's novels are analysed to explain the psychological roots of alienation. Man-woman relationship in its complexity is explored. Desai's novels echo the wailing of the feminine heart. *Cry, the Peacock* and *Where Shall We Go This Summer?* are, indeed, fictive metaphors of tension in togetherness.

And yet, there is another dimension of alienation that is existential. Arun Joshi's novels *The Foreigner* and *The Last Labyrinth* spell out the lower depths of human suffering and existential agony. This metaphysical dimension of alienation finds its congruent articulation in his fiction. Two novels each of three recent novelists Markandaya, Desai, Joshi and one novel of Kiran Desai have been selected to show the different facets of alienation and explore the theme of alienation in totality. It illustrates how literature and life are intrinsically inter-related. Fiction is not art for art's sake; it is forged in the smithy of human life and is not merely revealing but socially relevant too.

A word about the structure of the book. The book is designed to deal with the theme of alienation in some of the Indian English novels. The thesis is divided into six chapters. The first chapter which is the Introduction spells out the propriety of this study. In chapter two to five an endeavour has been made to study the theme of alienation in the novels of Kamala Markandaya, Anita Desai, Arun Joshi and Kiran Desai. Chapter six is the summing up of my study. A hope has been expressed here that sooner or later, reconciliation and rapprochement will take the place of alienation and isolation and world citizenship will prevail which will augur well for future. Acrimony, misunderstanding, disillusionment and loss of faith will be replaced by mutual trust, understanding, confidence and love.

At the end, I have added critical evaluations on Aravind Adiga's *The White Tiger* and Chetan Bhagat's *One Night @ the Call Centre*, the books which are of great topical interest. These explorations are intended to enhance the intrinsic value of Indian literature and culture.

Acknowledgement

First of all I thank the Almighty for giving me an opportunity to articulate my feelings before the sympathetic readers. I express my deep sense of gratitude to Dr. H. M. Prasad retd. Professor and Head of the Department of English, Magadh University, for his ready consent to guide and supervise my work. I owe my special debt to Dr. Gupteshwar Prasad, retd. Professor of English, Gaya College, Gaya, for his kind help and encouragement. I shall be remiss, if I fail to express indebtedness to my teachers, Dr. Nagendra Prasad, retd. Professor of English, M.U., Bodh Gaya, Dr. B.N. Sahay, retd. Professor and Head of the Department of English, M.U., and Dr. C.P. Singh, Professor and Head of the Department of English, M.U., for their constant help and invaluable guidance. I owe most cordial thanks to my husband, Dr. P. Shekhar for sustaining my interest in literary pursuits. I wish to record my indebtedness to Priya, Abhinav and Pranav for their unpretentious co-operation. I also owe a debt of gratitude to my brothers, sisters, brothers-in-law and sisters-in-law for their encouragement and help. I shall be failing in my duty if I do not thank Mr. B.P. Karan for composing this work with meticulous care. And last but not the least, I heartily thank a lot of persons, who have helped me directly or indirectly in completion of this work.

Introduction
The Agony of Alienation

> All order is gone out of my life . . . no peace, nothing to keep me within the pattern of familiar everyday living and doing that becomes those whom God means to live on earth. Thoughts come, incidents occur, and then they are scattered, and disappear. Past, present, future. Truth and untruth. They shuttle back and forth, a shifting chiaroscuro of light and shade. . . . Those are no longer my eyes, nor this my mouth. . . . The pattern forum order of lines and designs, a symmetry . . . has deserted my own life . . . strangers surround me.
> (Anita Desai, *Cry, the Peacock*)

Fiction is essentially a candid configuration of human reality assuming diverse forms. The cosmic epic of Henry James, the interior monologue of James Joyce, the fantasies of Kafka, the metaphoric travelogues of Saul Bellow, the symbolic parables of Hemingway or the metaphysical exploration of Raja Rao—all these are its different manifestation. In different times and in different cultures, they have given a complex fictive form to the contemporary social milieu. Indian fiction in English has also revealed deep concern with the changing facets of Indian life and reality. In its primary phase, it dealt with themes relating to rural life, the suffering and endurance of the peasants, the growing national consciousness, the emergence of industrialization and its impact on the sylvan world. A little later, related themes of freedom struggle, impact of Gandhism, partition and its after-effect, clash between tradition and modernity, east-west encounter and cultural clashes found expression in the varied works of different novelists. Mulk Raj Anand's *Untouchable*, R.K. Narayan's *Waiting for the Mahatama*, Raja Rao's *The Serpent and the Rope* are successful efforts in this direction. In the novels of such writers as Anand, Narayan, Kamala Markandaya, Bhabani Bhattacharya, Manohar Malgonkar, Nayantara Sahgal, Santha Rama Rao and

Ruth Prawer Jhabvala, realism, in one form or the other, remains the essential creed and life in its social context, the central concern.

In fact, Indian fiction realized various possibilities in the hands of Mulk Raj Anand, R.K. Narayan and Raja Rao. Anand's fiction has been shaped by what he himself calls 'the double burden on my shoulders, the Alps of the European tradition and the Himalaya of Indian past.' It is mainly from the Indian tradition that Anand derives his fervent socialism and his vision of modern egalitarian society. Anand's principal novels form an extended chronicle in which his social humanism finds a persistent expression in the form of humanitarian compassion for the low and the lost. *Untouchable*, *Coolie*, *Two Leaves and a Bud*, *The Village*, *Across the Black Water*, *The Sword and the Sickle* and *The Big Heart*—all these novels hinge around the axis of social problems inflicting the life of the poor, the low and the exploited. His fiction is an eloquent protest and a deep longing for ameliorating the sufferings of the common masses. The art of R.K. Narayan, standing as a sharp contrast to that of Anand, offers a delicate blend of gentle irony and sympathy, quiet realism and fantasy. His little dramas of middle class life, enacted in imaginary town, named Malgudi, cover in their sweep, the changing spectrum of Indian society, the political influence impinging on it and in their final implication they reflect modern India rooted in ancient tradition and caught up in the crucible of change.

Raja Rao's *Kanthapura* is a fine evocation of the Gandhian age in Indian English fiction. It is a brilliant attempt to probe "the depths to which the nationalistic urge penetrated showing how, even in the remote villages the new upsurge fused completely with traditional religious faith thus rediscovering the Indian soul."[1] It is a novel dealing with rural life. Like Hardy's *Far from the Madding Crowd*, and Premchand's *Godan*, *Kanthapura* takes us to a remote village far off from the din and bustle of urban life. The small village Kanthapura is situated in the far interior of Mysore in South India. Kanthapura is India in microcosm. What happens there, is precisely what happened everywhere in India during the appalling period of freedom movement, though the novel has nothing to do with Gandhi's non-cooperation movement or his peaceful struggle. The central character of the novel is Moorthy, a young, boisterous and enthusiastic fellow with dynamic views, who is determined to shake the village out of its complacency by his revolutionary ideas. Moorthy is a Brahmin by caste. But he is not caste ridden. As in Chaucer's *Canterbury Tales*, one here comes across variegated characters like Postmaster Surya Narayan, Patwari Nanjundist, Zamindar Bhatta, Patel Range Gowda, the peasant chief, also called 'The Tiger' and Moorthy, an idealist. Raja Rao is a master of characterization. He categorizes the tenets of his characters dispassionately from the standpoint of detached spectator. His characters are all real and life-size. They speak and act and think and feel as human beings and their angularities and passions are brought out with utmost vividness and clarity.

His later novels, *The Serpent and the Rope* and *The Cat and Shakespeare*, are profoundly philosophical and symbolic and in different ways they are metaphysical explorations into human reality. Bhabani Bhattacharya's novels *Music for Mohini*, *He Who Rides a Tiger*, *A Goddess Named Gold*, *Shadow from Ladakh*, and *A Dream in Hawaii* are spun around the themes of brutal famine, the confrontation between the Western and the Eastern values, the principles of Gandhism pitted against the shadow of War and the East-West encounter in its varied dimensions. Malgonkar's novels are neatly constructed narratives, which present rather limited view of life and human nature seen through the eyes of a hard-boiled man of the world.

The Indian novel in English, however, acquires a more complex and allusive dimension with the leading contemporary novelists like Kamala Markandaya, Anita Desai, Nayantara Sahgal, Arun Joshi and the more recent ones like Kiran Desai, Aravind Adiga and Chetan Bhagat.

To tell the truth, in its recent phase, the new fictional art has explored more contemporary problems of sex, conjugal clashes, cultural chaos, loss of identity and psychic dilemmas of individual characters. The recent novels have shifted their focus from the social phenomena to individual characters like their Western counterparts. The emergence of Anita Desai indicates the dawn of a new ethos in the history of Indian novels in English. She makes the contours of the inner weather of the mind and articulates most poetically the tension of man-woman relationship and the traumatic differences between them in the urban milieu. Anita Desai, Nayantara Sahgal, Arun Joshi, Nargis Dalal, Kamala Das, Mayah Balse, Ruth Prawer Jhabvala, Kamala Markandaya, Jhumpa Lahiri, Arundhati Roy, Kiran Desai, Aravind Adiga, Chetan Bhagat, to name a few, are the other emerging recent novelists. They reveal Indian life in urban conditions, which are distinctively Indian. Their problem is sometimes psychological, sometimes existential and sometimes moral. They mostly deal with the human and universal problem.

The twentieth century has been rightly called 'The Age of Alienation.' Modern man is fated to suffer the coercive impact of alienation. It manifests itself variously in the form of generation gap, the credibility of loss of gap, the compartmentalization of life, the stunning of personal development and the cessation of the sense of meaningfulness of life, etc. As Edmund Fuller puts it, "in our age, man suffers not only from war, persecution, famine and ruin, but from inner problem . . . a conviction of isolation, randomness, [and] meaninglessness in his way of existence."[2] The malaise of the contemporary man has been considerably aggravated by what Spengler calls 'the crisis of the present.' The present century has seen the dissolution of old certainties and, as Paul Brunton points out, "never before were so many people plunged in so much uncertainty, so much perplexity and unsettlement."[3]

The pervasive sense of alienation has corroded human life from various quarters. The modern man has shrunk in spirit languishing in confusion, frustration, disintegration, disillusionment and alienation. His very notion of reality has profoundly changed on account of Bergson's theory of duree, Freud's doctrine of the subconscious, Einstein's concept of relativity and Heisenberg's uncertainty principle. Consequently he suffers from an acute sense of rootlessness, which may manifest itself as 'the alienation from oneself, from one's fellowmen and from nature, the awareness that life runs out of one's hand like sand."[4]

The hiatus between what the individual aspires for and the harsh reality of what he achieves, what he professes and what he practises, what he realises and what he would like to be taken for, has crumpled his life leaving an insidious effect on his inner being. The injuries inflicted and the scars left on his psyche make him realize his helplessness. Angst-ridden and utterly hopeless, he finds life 'infinitely vast' without any proper 'linkage' to hold it together from falling apart. Painfully aware of his precarious position, man experiences today severe limitations arising out of randomness and alienation.

The plight of modern man has been discussed by Melvin Seemen under a set of five interrelated operational conditions, namely powerlessness, meaninglessness, normlessness, isolation and self-estrangement which are nothing but different manifestations of alienation. "These alternative meanings of alienation" as he puts it, "can be profitably applied in conjunction with one another in the analysis of a given state of affairs."[5] The most obvious repercussion of alienation can be seen in a person's fractured consciousness and his "fractionated functions"[6] There can be several layers and kinds of alienation, i.e. 'social alienation,' 'self-alienation,' 'cultural alienation,' 'linguistic alienation,' etc. Social alienation results from the sense of estrangement brought out by the sudden discovery that the social system is either oppressive or incompatible or incomplete with their desires and ideals. "Self-alienation, however, means the loss of contact of the individual selves with any inclinations or desires that are not in agreement with the prevailing social patterns as a result of which the individuals are forced to manipulate in accordance with the social demands or feel incapable of controlling their actions."[7] To be self-alienated thus means to be something less than one might ideally be if circumstances in society were conducive. Self-alienation seems to have worse effects on an individual than social, linguistic or cultural alienation. The former is the more basic form of rootlessness, and can thwart an individual's mental and psychic development in an alarming manner.

The theme of alienation and loneliness is a recurring theme in modern Western fiction. Consequently modern novel is an existential fable on man's predicament. The protagonist of Dostoievski is 'possessed'; Camus' is 'outsider,' Kafka's is under the 'trial,' Beckett's is 'absurd,' Bellow's is 'displaced' and Ellison's is 'invisible.' These tortured individuals are synoptic of the disinheritance of the Western life. The experience of disinheritance and futility has not percolated in the wide fabric of our Indian life, but it has pierced into the life of a significant segment of our society. Life in India is also no longer tranquil and composite. Life in our country is also changing fast and its changing facets are mirrored in Indian English novels. Kamala Markandaya, Anita Desai, Arun Joshi and Kiran Desai have given a fictional form to this new experience of the upper urban society. They have shown their awareness of the emerging dilemma of human loneliness, rootlessness, and an ardent sense of quest for one's identity are the *leit motif* of the fiction of Kafka, Sartre, Camus, Mann, Durrell, Saul Bellow and Malamud. Their protagonists grope in the labyrinths of existence; their dilemma is metaphysical. They are living metaphors of loneliness.

Kamala Markandaya's *The Nowhere Man*, *The Coffer Dams*, and *Possession* are novels written on the theme of immigration finally sublimating into the metaphysical dilemma of human isolation. *Possession*, Kamala Markandaya's fourth novel, also deals with the theme of loneliness and alienation. Here the scene shifts from India to England and America, and again back to India. It is the story of Valmiki, the great oriental artist whose art stifles in an alien country. He is unable to adjust himself in a foreign country, though he gains recognition, he loses his spontaneity. A rich aristocratic English woman, Lady Caroline Bell discovers a talent for painting in the south-Indian boy, Valmiki. She takes him to England to re-make him in her image of the great Indian artists. It is the *Pygmalion* theme. Valmiki becomes the artist, Lady Bell intends but at the expense of nearly destroying his soul. He finds only waste and death in personal relationship and to recover his true self he has to break with Lady Bell and come back to India.

This novel may be described as an allegory of the direction, independent India has to take on its onward march to progress. The story of Valmiki and Caroline Bell suggests that India has to draw sustenance from life-giving springs of its own culture. Valmiki is a rustic Indian artist; he is a symbol of the raw Independent India for the possession of whose soul, Caroline Bell, symbolizing the Western civilization, makes an all-out effort. Alienated from the spiritual roots of the country, Valmiki's artistic talents wither and smother. His final return to the Swami is suggestive of the reality that while a brief contact with the Western culture is useful, finally India's fulfillment lies in its own nourishing spiritual power.

In *The Coffee Dams*, feeling of alienation occurs due to culture displacement. The British are unable to adjust in the Indian culture and the natives with the English. The characters jostle between cross-cultural situations, ways of life and attitude of mind. Clinton is the typical representative of European technological civilization, who looks upon India as the vast sprawling enigma. He represents the ruthless efficiency of business-minded British engineers. The chief of the tribe symbolizes suffering and tension as well as underlying hope and faith of uprooted inhabitants of the hills. However, Helen and Bashiam symbolize the forces of moderation and human attitudes. Helen gets peace and fulfillment when she experiences her union with Bashiam.

Here the conflict is accentuated in real encounters between the Indian and English engineers. The English engineers came to India with memories of the colonial past. 'We like keeping ourselves to ourselves,' said Jackson. They proceed to build their little England "in the orderly scene . . . the trim square plots of emerging gardens, the gravelled paths, the white-washed boulders that demarcate and uphold private property rights."[8] They took precautions against the dangers of drinking polluted water and living in 'tiger country.' Fenced in securely, they believed that no good came out of associating with the Indians and believed in sticking together with the British. The Indians on their part kept away from the English because of their new-found independence and also because they were convinced of their culture being superior to those of the others. There were few occasions for them to meet socially and when the neutral Englishman associated with the Indians like Helen and Lefevere did, the others raged against them. The

Rawlings were appalled to see Lefevere bring Gopal Rao as a companion to their dinner. 'Look, what the lad's brought in,' cried Millie Rawlings and though her husband asked her not to make a scene about it, she discreetly refused to shake hands with Gopal Rao resorting to a 'namaste' instead.

Even though Clinton was the head of the operations, he had no idea where his Indian labourers came from or went into the trailing mountain paths into the jungle. The English who took pride in being well advanced in technical know-how, doubted whether the Indians would ever be able to acquire what was 'in the bone' of the Englishman. This gave them power over the Indians and fuelled their ego. It was further intensified by their economic solidity. They believed themselves to be the real 'Sahibs' and 'Mems' who shopped in the big city emporia. But they were wittingly 'flattered' by the Indian shopkeepers who really held them in contempt. They left behind the money cult which the tribal chief said would really be 'a peace full of mourning' for it would leave the tribals pining for trash. Neither the British accepted the Indians nor did the Indians accept the British. Kamala Markandaya's *The Nowhere Man* is a novel which reflects the dimension of alienation emerging from the trauma of immigration and cultural displacement. The novel treats the tragic life of an elderly Indian immigrant Srinivas. Even after having lived half a century in England, Srinivas is compelled to feel like an outsider, an outcaste. Srinivas spent his early youth in a small south Indian town in pre-independence days. But he and his wife, Vasantha, were forced to leave India, as their family was suspected of underground activities against the British rule in India. They settle down in England and later their two sons are born and brought up there. Vasantha's hope of selecting his son's wife is shattered when Lakshman marries Pat, an Englishwoman. Her dream of living together with her sons is also shattered. Broken, she dies of consumption rendering Srinivas utterly lonely.

One day Srinivas meets an elderly divorcee named Mrs. Pickering. Srinivas invites her to share his house with him. She starts living with him. She helps him rehabilitate himself. But, finally he becomes a victim of racialism. Fred Fletcher, his neighbour, torments Srinivas in several ways. He, however, does not react. Instead he becomes introspective. He sadly reflects upon his rootlessness. He is compelled to consider himself a nowhere man, an alien despite his stay for fifty years in England and despite his sons having laid down their lives for the country. While in a fit of depression, he contemplates committing suicide but Mrs. Pickering prevents him from doing so. He also gets afflicted with leprosy. Although he undergoes treatment, he decides to isolate himself. He asks his tenants to leave his place, not because he is anti-white but because he is a leper and this worsens the situation. Fred sets fire to Srinivas' building but ironically he himself perishes in the fire. Srinivas is saved but dies of shock. Both the hater and the hated are destroyed. The alien remains the alien. *The Nowhere Man* in its final evaluation is a fable of human isolation.

Anita Desai is another major novelist who explores the anguish of alienation but in her case alienation emerges from psychic tension. She is a novelist of the inner mind and probes into the tortured self of the sensitive women, who fail to adjust to the cruel, insensitive male counterparts. Man-woman relationship in the urban society is her concern and in novel after novel, she gives deep configuration to this dilemma.

Her first novel, *Cry, the Peacock* (1963), is a trend setting novel as it deals with the psychical rather than with physical aspects of its characters in sheer poetic terms. If Meena Belliappa found in it "a remarkable attempt to fuse, fantasy with perpetual experience,"[9] Darshan Singh Maini places it next to Raja Rao's book, *The Serpent and the Rope* 'the most poetic and evocative Indo-Anglican novel."[10] The novel chiefly deals with the strange obsessions of the hypersensitive heroine Maya who kills her husband Gautama by pushing him off the parapet and then commits suicide too. Marriage between Maya and Gautama was a marriage of convenience. Maya a pampered daughter of a wealthy Brahmin is married to Gautama, a rather insensitive, pragmatic and rational advocate, who fails to understand her sensitive nature. She suffers from father obsession and looks for a father image in her husband. In her childhood, an albino astrologer had predicted that four years after her marriage, one of them would die and the prediction eats up the vitals of her soul and makes her obsessed with the fear of death. As an after-thought, she realizes that one of the two could be Gautama as well and she kills him by pushing him off the parapet. The tragedy results from the lack of communication and lack of the merger of the self.

In her second novel *Voices in the City* (1965), the city of Kali, Calcutta, acquires the form of a powerful character. That is why Madhusudan Prasad calls it "an epic on Calcutta."[11] Three major characters Nirode, Monisha and Amla are depicted as questers in search of proper vocation and proper moorings. The novel is divided into four sections—named after each character—'Nirode,' 'Monisha,' 'Amla,' and 'Mother.' They deal respectively with the failures of a Bengali youth Nirode, the troubled life of Monisha, the commercial art of Amla and the indifferent attitude of their mother. Nirode and his two sisters Monisha and Amla are rebels against the solid conventions of middle-class life and long for creativity and self-expression. Each comes to grief: Nirode ends up as a drifting Bohemian, Monisha commits suicide and Amla is heart-broken when her love is rejected. As Nirode's basic needs have been frustrated, he alienates himself from his essential nature; his value system is damaged. He accepts neurotic values, thereby developing neurotic wants, which are destructive, both for self and for others.

Fears of personal inferiority lead Nirode to search glory, first by being an outlaw and then by priding himself as an 'ill-tempered hermit.' In real life, he cannot be at par with his brother Arun, neither in academic field nor in extra-curricular activities. This is insulting. He feels unwanted, isolated and belittled. The unconscious mental process devise, ways and means to surmount his inadequacy. As a boy, he achieves this by running away from home several times. Being searched for and brought back home elevate his position in his own eyes. That he belongs to them, that he is wanted, is in itself an anxiety relieving feeling. Thus, he manages to get that much-needed parental attention, which he otherwise fails to attract.

Nirode's chaotic state of mind indicates the terror of the dark unknown, Death. He tells Amla that he has been sentenced to death. 'I am prepared and waiting for it. I have heard her approach—death, Kali . . . while she watches I grow more and more vividly alive by the minute and also closer and closer to my death." Nirode recognizes the duality; knowledge and ignorance, reality and illusion, good and evil, life and death. Likewise he is himself rent by the contradictions of his life, the struggles between his two selves—real and idealized.

A psychological evaluation of Nirode's character scores the fact that he is a representative of the sickness of contemporary existence which fails to give a unified sense of experience to the artist.

It is an 'existential' novel that explores the inner climate of youthful despair, epitomized by her over-acutely self-conscious Nirode, that quoter of Camus, finding no meaning in his own life or in life at all. This existential 'angst' is duplicated in Monisha, in whom it assumes a fatal rhythm from which Nirode was once narrowly saved but which in her reaches its inevitable end. Calcutta appears to accentuate and even to embody the despair of oversensitive souls. No consolation can be found in the traditional Indian institutions, of marriage, joint families or even in Indian culture—the rich musical, artistic and literary culture of Bengal. Marriage is a tomb for Monisha, an institution despised by her aunt and by the scientist, Rita, who abandons marriage for a career. For the three who narrate the story, their parents' unhappy marriage is a bleak warning. Anita Desai's tortured characters are thus robbed of traditional consolations. Each man or woman has to make his own life and face his inevitable fate. Each is alone in the terrible city of death.

Bye-Bye, Blackbird (1971) is the only novel of Anita Desai in which social and political realities take precedence over probing of the mind. The novel mirrors alienation and lack of adjustment encountered by Indian immigrants in England. Dev feels alienated in London from both Indians and Englishmen because the former have become used to the condescending attitude of the natives which he cannot do, and the latter consider him an outsider. Happy in the beginning, Adit begins to feel alienated later on. He does not appreciate 'this business of always hanging together with people like ourselves, all wearing the label 'Indian Immigrants,' never daring to try and make contact outside this circle.' Sarah too suffers a great deal, even if inwardly, as she, by marrying an Indian, becomes alienated in her own country. Adit notices in Sarah 'an anguish . . . of loneliness.'

Adit Sen in *Bye-Bye, Blackbird* is an Indian, who lives in England. Having been taught from childhood to appreciate the British history and literature, ways and manners, he reconciles to his stay in England and suffers humiliation ungrudgingly, though identifying himself inwardly with India which is quite obvious in his longing for Indian friends, activities, food, dress, music, news and stories. Thus initially he finds no problem in adjusting in England. Sarah, his English wife, finds by hints and suggestions that she is not liked by her own countrymen for having married an Indian. Adit and Sarah love each other even though their language, taste, likes and dislikes continue to differ. Sarah cooks Indian curry without developing taste for it while Adit has no taste for some British items of food. Sarah's cat does not please Adit. Sarah does not like Indian music, nor can she understand and appreciate Indian jokes and conversation which Adit enjoys a great deal. People deride her by calling "Mrs. Skurry." Caught between two cultural currents, Sarah acts two different roles and fears losing her identity.

In *Where Shall We Go This Summer?* Anita Desai dramatizes two opposite conflicts. The protagonist is a nervous sensitive, middle-aged woman. She finds herself alienated from her husband and children. This sense of alienation is because of her emotional imbalance. The unhappy part of her life is due to her inability to accept the values and mode of attitudes of her society. She feels dullness, boredom and deadness in every individual. And these are the greatest threat to her individuality. Sita is sensitive, peace-loving and introvert. The tension in the novel is between a sensitive individual and an insensitive world conveyed through the most frequently recurring image of the predator and the prey. Using the method of objective correlative, Anita Desai portrays Sita's condition by describing the plight of an eagle as it is surrounded and harassed by the crows. She wanted to fight against the crows with a gun, stones, even a toy gun to help the eagle but could not. Raman asks Sita to leave the Manori island and to go back and she obediently returns.

The novel, structurally divided into three parts, narrates the story of Sita, its middle-aged heroine. She resents her fifth pregnancy. In order not to give birth to her child by revoking the magic, she goes to Manori, her maiden home. Her stay on the island awakens her to life's reality, and she chooses to accept the routine of her existence. Sita's mental, moral and emotional issues oscillate between the two polarities of 'yes' and 'no.' This compromise with life is gained after a prolonged period of intrapsychic conflicts. Sita shifts from compliance to rebellion and then to withdrawal, again coming back to compliance. Since she vacillates between her changing strategies, her behaviour is inconsistent and leaves much scope for disparity between her thinking and actions. In the first part of the novel, entitled, "Monsoon 67," she rebels against her family and decides to go to Manori, 'What I'm doing is trying to escape from the madness here, escape to a place where it might be possible to be sane again.'[12] In the vehemence and spite of her bellicosity, there appears no redemption for her from the madness. The second part "Winter 47" depicts Sita's life twenty years back, her life with her father. Here we can see her development as a compliant person. This part enables us to understand her later conflicts. Raman visits the island to fetch his children. Sita too decides to accompany him. Personally she reconciles with her situation. Socially, she is dubbed 'mad' by Moses and his friends.

Sita's condition is just the reverse of Maya's in *Cry, the Peacock*. If Maya's father is over-protective, Sita's father neglects her completely. Sita is a motherless child. She experiences neglect and uncertainties right through her childhood. Her father, a public figure, admired and revered by the people, is too far-off and formidable a person for Sita to approach with filial affection.

Fire on the Mountain (1977), Desai's fifth novel, is the winner of Sahitya Akademi Award besides several other prizes and awards. It won the Royal Society of Literature's Winfred Hartley Memorial Prize and in 1978 National Academy of Letters award.

The statesman considered it "an outstanding novel . . . Sharp and refined, descriptive as well as symbolic." Through this novel, Desai gives us a positive message, very valuable in the context of contemporary society. She gives us a chance to try to strike a balance between reality and illusion and to make our life more meaningful. Here she highlights the truth that a life of undiluted reality or undiluted illusion spells tragedy. Nanda Kaul and Ila Das are such characters whose existentialist problems are unsolved. Nanda Kaul feeds herself on illusions. But when she receives the tragic news of the rape and murder of Ila Das, her illusions change into reality. On the contrary, Ila Das faces real life. Nanda Kaul, an old woman, has had too much of the world with her and so, longs for a quiet, retired life. She desperately desires to avoid familiar obligations around her, so she withdraws determinedly into Carignano, her hill-side home in Kasauli where she hopes to live a radiantly single life. Nanda Kaul does not welcome the news of the arrival of her great grand-daughter Raka visiting her. Raka also feels miserable like a caged bird, a wild animal tamed and domesticated. Though they live under the same roof physically, emotionally they are miles apart. Theirs is a strange living together, each resenting and avoiding the presence of the other. If the old lady loves to live alone, the young Raka desires it no less but with a certain difference. Then we have Ila Das, a piano teacher-turned-social worker who also breaks in Nanda Kaul's solitude. Her voice is enough to disturb Nanda Kaul's life. In fact, Ila Das is a noble soul struggling against the odds of life. She is aware of the facts of life that misery and suffering are inevitable in life. However, for her good intentions, she is assaulted and raped under the cover of darkness. The telephonic news of her death results in the death of Nanda Kaul. This tragedy leaves Raka utterly alone.

The picture of life that Anita Desai presents in this novel is no doubt dismal but it is the truth of life. Human life has so many facets and there are different angles from which it can be viewed and reviewed. Here the protagonist Nanda Kaul is no longer a young woman trying to find a place for her self in an adult setting or relate to a new family structure. She is rather a woman of mature years who has experienced different situations and relationships and who has succeeded in fulfilling their claims. In worldly terms, she has been a giver all her life, holding back only the hour of stillness every after noon. But with the children grown and settled and her husband dead, she has moved to Carignano, away from the activity of life.

The central chapters that describe Raka's self finding through the exploration of the hillside are the best in the book, and Nanda's and Ila's viperous sense of loneliness and alienation is also brought out convincingly. The supreme irony is that Nanda with all her children, grandchildren and great grandchildren and the unmarried Ila equally feel utterly lonely, which is meant to show up the futility of living, married or single.

Desai's *Clear Light of Day* can be treated as a four-dimensional novel. The anguish of a sensitive young woman caught between movement and stillness has been rendered here in this novel like a musical piece of work. The novel begins with the song of a koel and ends with the song of the old master. In a sense, the novel is about the growth of four children of a family in an absurd surrounding. Two young girls Bim and Tara grow up. Their parents are indifferent and disinterested. They have to cope with a diabetic mother, careless father and a mentally retarded brother. Besides this, they have the responsibility of tending to a young tubercular brother and an alcoholic old aunt. Thus, they have to live in an absurd world where indifference, disease and irrationality seem to thwart all normal human responses. This domestic drama of absurdity takes place against the background of partition of the country. It suggests another pattern of violence, bloodshed and absurdity. The death of their parents makes the children emotionally destitute. Tara, the younger girl, gets married and goes abroad with her husband. Raja, the elder of the two brothers, gets married to the daughter of his Muslim neighbour Haider Ali. He leaves Delhi and settles down in Hyderabad. Thus Bim is left to look after the domestic affairs including the mentally deficient, old and infirm Baba.

The novelist picks up the story at a point where Tara and her husband Bakul are visiting home after a considerable lapse of time. They have come in anticipation of the wedding of Raja's daughter Moyna. This incident provides an opportunity to see the action from the dual perspective of past and present. The juxtaposition of the past and the present, the near and the remote, the subjective and the objective suggests the theme of continuity in change. It keeps us alive to the changing dimensions of reality.

In part two of the novel, the novelist portrays life in Delhi during the partition in 1947 with horror of communal riots, suspense, sensation and terrorist activities. The portrait of aunt Mira adds to the novel a new dimension of deep pathos. She is terribly ill with a strange disease. She falls in fits twice or thrice a day. Her last hysterical fit is symbolic of her obsession with the image of well.

Part three of the novel delineates some significant events in the early life of Bim. Tara and Raja before 1947 with which part two of the novel is linked.

Part four of the novel shows Desai's art of skilful structure and reflects time as fourth dimension. Bim and Tara's conversation is marked with appreciable change. However, Bim's attitude changes and she is repentant of her wrong attitude towards Raja. Her misconception disappears paving the way for her to see everything by "the clear light of day.' She is also reminded of Eliot's famous line, "time the destroyer is time the preserver."

Baumgartner's Bombay (1988), consisting of seven chapters, alternatively focuses on the past and present of the two isolated Germans without family and country. Hugo Baumgartner, the protagonist, is the central character and the other is a female cabaret dancer, Lotte, whose presence gets a secondary importance. But the stories of these two characters run parallel.

The novel opens with Baumgartner, a German Jew, living out his final years in solitude in a shabby flat behind the Taj Hotel in Bombay. He has been in India for a period of fifty years and the happiness in expectation of which he comes to Bombay remains unfulfilled. He is living a solitary life with none to look after him. The only company is that of cats that he nurses and loves. Both Baumgartner and Lotte are sailing in the same boat of isolation in an alien country, among their memories and dreams.

Looking back at the past life of Baumgartner, one finds him a young German who came to India for starting a new life in business. He was forced to leave Germany fifty years ago, when violence had broken out during the Nazi Germany. Hugo's father Herr Baumgartner was a wealthy furniture dealer and a man of authority, pride and status in Berlin. With the sudden death of his father, Hugo's schooling came to an end. At the suggestion of the gentleman from Hamburg, Hugo was sent to India to do timber business and to start a new life. The first place he came to was Bombay. But in the new atmosphere, Baumgartner got nothing but loneliness and isolation. Later he shifted to Calcutta. Here too his life did not remain peaceful for a long time. The war had broken out and he was arrested and was taken to a detention camp in Ahmednagar where the aliens like him from all over the country were kept. Baumgartner was kept a captive there for six years. The expectations of happiness in the business got totally blurred as the lonely prison life threw him in a state of isolation.

With the end of the war, Baumgartner's life in prison also came to an end and he met Habibullah, his old friend, who suggested to him to go back to his life of timber business. It was a time when the riots had started and it was not safe for Habibullah, a Muslim to pursue his business. At the suggestion of Habibullah, he decided to go to Bombay as it was safer for him to do some business there.

There he met Chimanlal, who let out a small flat to him at a reasonable rate behind Taj Hotel. At his instruction, Baumgartner started transport business. Baumgartner found a new work and prosperity in Bombay and an unexpected flair for success at the race track. There he met Lotte again after so many years. Both of them were overjoyed to see each other after a long time. The pre-war conditions that had separated them in an unexpected way brought them closer all of a sudden. Both the isolated characters that were now old consoled each other. During such moments, Lotte would confess to Baumgartner that they should have gone back to their country long back instead of living here as isolated foreigners. Even after staying here for such a long time, both of them felt isolated and cut off from the mainstream of Indian life.

But the story does not end here. The story of Baumgartner takes a tragic turn. One day, Farrokh, the waiter in cafe De Paris, informed Baumgartner about a young German named Kurt who was sitting in the café with his face towards the wall, and was hostile to everyone. Baumgartner, who was isolated but contented with the mild pleasures of old age, tried to befriend the young man in order to overcome his loneliness. This became the cause of his tragic death as he was murdered by Kurt. After the death of Baumgartner, Lotte remains an isolated figure, totally broken after losing her oldest friend.

Alienation in its diverse aspects is the recurrent theme in Arun Joshi's novels. His heroes are intensely self-centred persons prone to self-pity and escapism. In spite of their weaknesses, they are, however, genuine seekers who grope towards a purpose in life and self-fulfillment. The central image of all his novels is of foreigner. His characters are not merely in Jamesian dilemma of dual cultures, but they are walking metaphors of alienation—a Sindi Oberoi who is a foreigner wherever he goes, a Billy Biswas retreating to the primitive world to find life essence in Bilasia, a Ratan Rathor torn between guilt and confession or finally a Som Bhaskar lost in the labyrinth of death and life, existence and reality, doubt and faith, Darwin and Krishna.

Sindi Oberoi in *The Foreigner* (1968) is a born 'foreigner' a man alienated from all humanity. The only son of an Indian father and an English mother, born in Kenya, he is orphaned at an early age and grown into a youth without family ties and without a country. 'My foreignness lay within me,' he confesses. Educated in England and USA, he sums up his life as 'twenty five years largely wasted in search of wrong things in wrong places.' He develops a philosophy of detachment, which is really a mask for his fear of committing himself; of getting involved too deeply with others. His love for an American girl, June Blyth, ends tragically both for the girl and for his best friend, Babu, primarily because Sindi [a short for 'Surrinder'] is afraid of marriage and its demands, 'of possessing anybody and . . . of being possessed.' He returns to India and joins an industrial concern but his rootlessness persists. Finally, when the numerous employees of his factory face ruin as a result of the exposure of the fraudulent boss, he discovers his latent humanitarianism, which compels him to save them by taking over the management.

The Strange Case of Billy Biswas (1971) presents the protagonist alienated from the higher middle-class society in which he is born and brought up and in which he is compelled to live, though he finds in himself an over-powering urge to march to a different drum altogether. Right from his adolescence, Billy has been conscious of a great force—a primitive force within himself, which continues to register its presence time and again. His higher training in anthropology in the U.S.A. accentuates this consciousness further. After his return to India, marriage and a secure teaching job in a major University fail to stifle the nagging, strident primitive voice within, and Billy runs away during an anthropological survey expedition to join a primitive tribe, where he is soon accepted as an incarnation of a legendary ancient king. The 'short happy life' of Billy Biswas ends when, during an attempt by his near relations to reclaim him, he is shot dead accidentally by a policeman.

The most acute kind of alienation is from our own self and in *The Apprentice* (1974) the hero Rathor, a minor Government official, is a victim. The son of a middle class freedom fighter, he had been a poet and an athlete in youth and his ambition had been to be good. 'Respected! To be of use! The imperatives of making a living, however, compel him to be a clerk and the prevailing atmosphere of corruption and mammonism in the post-Independence period soon corrodes his soul. His part in a fraudulent deal involving defective army supplies which leads to the death of his brigadier friend in the Sino-Indian war proves an eye-opener. Rathor's penance in his quest to regain his pre-lapsarian innocence, however, takes a form more symbolic than practical; he takes to polishing the shoes of the devotees who visit the temple on his way to his office.

The Last Labyrinth illumines fresher perspectives on the earlier novels because apart from carrying their genesis, it explores the anguish of alienation and the intensity of quest with great force and complexity. The story is about a plastic magnate and millionaire Som Bhaskar, married to Geeta and the father of two children, who meets enigmatic Anuradha who lives in Benaras with the decadent Aftab, and wants to possess the woman and buy the man's business. The story is about Som's misadventure with this dark and terrible love, and the 'labyrinth' symbolism is spread out all over. Lal haveli, Aftab's 'sepulchral, sensual den,' is located 'amidst the labyrinths of Benaras.' There are labyrinthine rooms and passages but what is the 'last' labyrinth? "Why, death of course!" is the 'labyrinth' a make-believe or a trap of fatality. Som is caught in the intricacies of the mysterious web, the flight of steps to Gargi Mata's room is a labyrinth too, and there is a labyrinth in the tobacco-stand house on hills; Som's half-hysterical half-fatalistic pursuit of Anuradha, losing her, gaining her, and losing her again. Besides Som and Anuradha, there is Aftab, his Azizum, and his factotum, Tarakki; and there is the God-Woman Gargi, and 'Krishna' the unpredictable God. What happens in the end? Anuradha saves Som from certain death by vowing to Gargi to give up her lover.

Kiran Desai's first novel, *Hullabaloo in the Guava Orchard* is not directly concerned with isolation and alienation. But undoubtedly, the seeds of isolation and alienation are found latent in this novel which is germinated in her second famous novel, *The Inheritance of Loss*. The seeds of the theme of alienation and isolation can be traced in the novel, *Hullabaloo in the Guava Orchard* in as much as it intends to bring out the clash between fanaticism and scientific attitude to life showing that where such a chasm takes place it is usually the former that triumphs over the latter. Man is constantly busy in the exploration of his identity and his endeavour turns futile because he is tagged to the age-old taboos and superstitions. He can realize his self only if he understands his environment lest he should be cut off from his own self.

Kiran Desai, the daughter of the eminent Indian English novelist Anita Desai, won 'Man Booker Prize' in 2007 for her novel *The Inheritance of Loss*. The novel is concerned with the theme of alienation the other way round. The story of the novel is partly set against the background of India and partly against the background of U.S.A. The characters portrayed in this novel are Indian, but they feel wholly alienated in their own motherland. They live like westerners in India. Laila and Noni are fine examples of this. They have so integrated the cultural effects of British colonization that in every bit of their gestures, they are non-Indian. Jemubhai is born in Pilphit, a Gujarat town near Baroda, goes to England and succeeds in the I.C.S examination. When he comes back to India, he becomes a stranger to himself and forgets to laugh. For five years, he fails to make a single friend. He sits all alone in his library, feeling completely cut off from society. No one speaks to him. Unable to cope with the conflict of identities, he is consumed by self-loathing. He develops an instinctive dislike for his heritage. He even hates the wheatish colour of his skin. In the end, he barely feels human at all. He is turned into a ridiculous Indian. His heart is frozen and he abhors his fellow Indians. He is cut off from his family and community. The memory of his old life style, like powdering his face, haunts his mind and he feels a kind of peculiar isolation and alienation. Biju, the son of the judge's cook, Panna Lal, illegally migrates to New York, works there in a fancy restaurant and enters a multi-cultural microcosm based on exploitation. He comes across people he is not aware of. He also meets Indians and Pakistanis there. He wishes he were young so that he might have thought of going back to India, his own country. But it is too late.

The agony of the westernized Indian, in search of identity, is well brought out by Kiran Desai in her novel, *The Inheritance of Loss*. Every Indian, whether of high rank or at the pedestal is put to a position where he quarrels with himself. He is constantly in search of his identity. Though he lives in his own country, he is literally a foreigner here. Mentally, he is so much isolated and alienated that he can hardly be called an Indian.

NOTES

1. M.K. Naik, *A History of Indian English Novel* (Sahitya Akademi, New Delhi, 1982), p. 167.
2. Qtd. *Indian Women Novelists*, ed. R.K. Dhawan (Prestige Books, New Delhi), 1991, Vol. II, p. 12
3. *The Spiritual Crisis of Man*, London, 1952, Qtd. *Indian Women Novelists* (Prestige, New Delhi), p. 7.

4. Erich Fromm et. al., *Zen Buddhism and Psychoanalysis* (New York, 1970), p. 86.
5. "On the Meaning of Alienation," *American Sociological Review* 24, 6 December 1959, p. 789.
6. Frank Johnson, ed., *Alienation: Concept, Term and Meaning* (New York and London, 1973), p. 46.
7. I. Travis, "Change in the Form of Alienations," *American Sociological Review*, 34/1 February 1969, pp. 46-47.
8. Kamala Markandaya, *The Coffer Dams* (Hind Pocket Books, Delhi, 1970), p. 11.
9. Meena Belliappa, *Anita Desai, A Study of Her Fiction* (Writers' Workshop, Calcutta, 1971).
10. Darshan Singh Maini, "The Achievement of Anita Desai," *Indo-English literature*, ed. K.K. Sharma (Vimal, Ghaziabad), p. 217.
11. Madhusudan Prasad, *Anita Desai: The Novelist* (New Horizon, Allahabad, 1981).
12. Anita Desai, *Where Shall We Go This Summer?* (Orient Paperback, Delhi, 1982), p. 35.

The Trauma of Deculturation in Kamala Markandaya's *The Coffer Dams* and *The Nowhere Man*

> It is time when one is made to feel unwanted, and liable, as a leper, to be ostracized further perhaps beyond the limit one can reasonably accept one self. (Kamala Markandaya, *The Nowhere Man*)

A potent facet of Indian social life is multiculturalism. No country can afford to insulate itself against the currents of social change at the global level. And in case of India, the interaction with the west is palpable. Consequently, cultural interaction, in its varied forms of acculturation, deculturation and assimilation, has formed a recurring and significant theme in Indian English novel. One of the fall-outs of cultural interaction is deculturation or cultural incompatibility. Kamala Markandaya has explored this experience of incommunication emerging from cultural heterogeneity in her several novels, namely, *Some Inner Fury*, *Possession*, *The Coffer Dams*, *The Nowhere Man, Pleasure City*, *The Golden Honeycomb* and *Two Virgins,* with wonderful insight and understanding. In this chapter, however, an attempt has been made to make an intensive study of *The Coffer Dams* and *The Nowhere Man*. These two novels, put together, complete the picture, in the former a group of westerners are shown in a typically rural Indian setting and in the latter, the story of an Indian family in London is etched out.

In fact, Kamala Markandaya is a major novelist who has projected the image of India in its various phases, before and after, independence, its tradition and change, its modernity, its rural, sylvan surroundings as well as modernization and technology. But what is most striking in her novel is the fact that cultural alienation forms the matrix of her vision. In all her novels, Markandaya explores the impact of change in terms of human psychology. To her, culture means essentially an idea which unites a million individuals and confers on each of them what Trilling calls integral selfhood.

The quintessence of Markandaya's novels lies in a fictive exploration of the human self in the context of complex cultural values. The reasons for this complex vision are manifold. Her predicament of being an Indian writer who has ample exposure to dual culture is further intensified by her personal life history. Born in Madras in an educated Brahmin family, she got her education at Madras University; she married an English man and settled in England. Kamala Markandaya's own life becomes relevant to the shaping of complex vision of the novelist. The themes of uprootedness, racial tension and prejudice, primitivism and technology, a search for one's true self, the experience of exile and alienation are seminal in her fiction writing. All these ring with the unmistakable strain of autobiography because living under alien sky, she is fully aware of the conflict between Eastern and Western values which enables her to portray India objectively from a distance.

The Coffer Dams is an ambitious novel and here the novelist jostles a throng of British and Indian characters into cross cultural situations, ways of life and attitude of mind. Clinton is the typical representative of European technological civilization who looks upon India as the vast sprawling enigma. He represents the ruthless efficiency of business-minded British Engineers. The chief of the tribe symbolizes suffering and tension as well as underlying hope and faith of uprooted inhabitants of the hills. However, Helen, Clinton's wife and Bashiam, the chief of the tribe symbolize the forces of moderation and human attitudes. Helen gets peace and fulfillment when she experiences her union with Bashiam. For the first time in her life she feels a sense of belongingness and a sense of universal inclusiveness. Helen and Bashiam represent blends of culture and the indispensable human links. Helen tries to seek fulfillment and her true identity in an alien country. British officers and technicians in general look upon India as an enigma:

From within the invisible white stockade thus thrown up, the new colonists peered at the vast sprawling enigma that they felt

India to some, like Clinton, with a total lack of interest, some, like

> Helen Clinton, with a great, consuming curiosity and effortless identification; some uneasily, reluctant to advance into territory whose strange codes and values made them as pigeons roosting on anti pigeon gully but most of them with rising tides of superiority lined and laced and made heady by fear, a nameless unvoiced fear that to step outside was hazard whose culmination would be a total, terrifying absorption of identity in an unknown ocean.[1]

The British characters, by and large, take pride in keeping close to themselves. They do not want any communication with outsiders. Jackson remarks: "We like keeping ourselves to ourselves." (37) Even young persons like Lefevere who were born in a period that looked sardonically on the empires and were not allowed to form any prejudice, find it easier to retreat within their own charmed circle. Women like Millie have a positive hatred for Indians. They vent their anger and venom on the country over trifles. The strain and inconvenience Rawlings had to undergo in transporting the cranes to the site make Rawlings curse himself for "slaving away at a thankless job in a thankless bloody country." (87) Clinton describes it as the blasted country and Mac Kendrick wonders, "God knows why . . . why we insist on carrying the white man's burden." (166) The memory of the days of the British Raj in India disturbs Mr. Rawlings because he finds it difficult to exploit the native:

> But it would not be same, he said, this country, where something has gone bloody wrong and the spirit is different and trace it down to the freedom which he believed has been delivered on plate. (192)

Indian officers are equally hostile to the British. Krishnan, the harsh-faced engineer, who dominates the group, rebuffs Helen when she expresses her surprise at fly-away foundations on which hill tribesmen build their whole lives:

> Of course they seem flying away to you, you are used to better things, unfortunately our people are not. They have become used to being done out of their rights. (43)

The rivalry between the British and Indian characters in this novel is not just incidental. It is purposeful. Such a juxtaposition of attitudes would have been a facile prosaic imposition on the body of the novel. But Kamala Markandaya imparts a fictional reality to it. She is a competent artist who spells out the landscape of the novel with the genuine experience of the characters. The clash in attitudes is a key to the conflict on the cultural level.

The novel centres around the construction of a dam named Coffer Dam to control and canalize the turbulent river in a hilly region somewhere in south India. Clinton and Mackendrick are the Chief Engineers who were bent upon completing the dam against innumerable obstacles caused by nature and also by the hostile attitude of Indian technicians and workers. Clinton is a typically western man, rational, confident and committed to his technological competence. He will construct the dam against all odds and pressures, even at the cost of humanitarian values. Being a man of steel, he will not listen to an opposition, to any delay in a schedule. In a system of business ethics and technological temper, no human values, no human emotions, can find any relevance. During the construction of the dam, two accidents take place. The first is the death of Bailey and Wilkins. The work is suspended to give them a decent Christian burial. Secondly, forty two Indians fall into the river and their dead bodies cannot be recovered because a boulder has jammed them. The attitude of Clinton to the work of recovering the dead bodies clearly shows his philosophy of life. He believes that instead of delaying the work, the bodies could be incorporated into the structure. The dialogues among Clinton, Helen, and Mackendrick portray Clinton as a perfect symbol of Western technological culture:

> 'But if it means pushing,' said Helen, and stumbled over words, which his kindness has done. 'It would be easy, if they were not, but they are men. If they are pushed it is a killing pace,' she said, sweat running.
>
> 'You think so yourself. I would not,' said Mackendrick, and thought of the years that she lacked, during which a callusing took place, which one called experience, being too dishonest to give it other names. I would not go as far as that, he said. (123)

Clinton turns down the demand as unreasonable. "I don't understand," he says, "such preoccupation over something which is lifeless and irrelevant, when there is so much at stake." (181)

The cynical arrogance with which Clinton refuses to accommodate the Indian sentiments about dead bodies is symbolic of British abhorrence for Indian values and is a significant point. Technology leaves no scope for human feelings and thus the western culture which is so technological in spirit cannot understand and assimilate essentially human qualities of Indian culture. This situation is indicative of the truth that the British and Indians cannot have permanent positive relationships if the technological spirit is not tempered with human virtues. The possibility of assimilation of two cultures is there. It is also suggestive of the collective sense of guilt which the white people have against India. Clinton's attitude is an index to the fact that behind the apparent coolness and indifference of the English, there is a sense of guilt about their violation of Indian spirit in the name of technological and material progress. This culminates in the scene when Millie runs amuck into the jungle and faints. Her madness is a moral allegory in as much as it configurates the collective guilt of the Europeans in the Eastern culture. Millie's flight into the jungle reminds us of the flight of O'Neill's Emperor Jones which was also an expression of the collective racial guilt.

Clinton can be seen essentially as a builder since he is all against destruction. But the irony is that the dam he builds brings about separation and gaps rather than ties and unities. In spite of his distaste for destruction, Clinton risks the death of a whole community for the sake of his proposed project. "It is a calculated risk," he said, "as sometimes one is forced, which one has to take since there is no other way." (216) When the river is in spate and the areas where tribals reside are in danger of being flooded, he refuses to breach the coffers. He is all the time under the spell of this fact. "I am a builder. We make the calculations; it is they who run the risk." (215) The dam, which already bore his name, the conception and completion of which had long back been visualized by him, he refused to trace back.

Clinton is presented with too much of individualistic ego motivated by a kind of ambition that transcends the materials. He embodies the force of ambition and his wife personifies the force of humanity motivated in two different directions, two viewpoints of equal magnitude are presented. Their relationship is incompatible. They are alienated from each other just like Gautama and Maya in Anita Desai's *Cry, the Peacock*. Clinton, like Gautama, is materialistic and Helen, like Maya, lives for passion. Helen expresses her feelings thus:

> It was as if they were walking on different levels, he on the overpass, she on the under. He had, as he said an overall vision. She saw the details, and the birds and the passions below. We on our different ways, she thought, and may be his is as valid as mine: but could not drum up much conviction and it remained an intellectual exercise. (11)

The novel reveals its real meaning if one tries to explicate the triangle of relationships among Clinton, Helen and Bashiam. In the beginning, Clinton and Helen are quite happy. They have mutual respect for each other. But slowly Helen is alienated from Clinton and she begins to assert her independent self. Helen learns the native dialect and is sympathetic with the Indian workers. She is an example of the new generation of sensitive and sympathetic English characters. In her friendship with natives, she discovers natural springs of social intercourse that promotes her cultural consciousness. Right from the beginning she is a character with a difference. Finding her husband in different human misery she asks him in despair, "Cannot you care? Don't human beings matter anything to you? Do they have to be special kind of flesh before they do?" (105)

Helen's bitter invective against modern European civilization finds its expression in her indignant outburst before Bashiam:

> The land, our instincts. The people who work in our factories, they've forgotten what fresh air is like. Our animals—we could learn from them but we're Christians you know, an arrogant people, so we deprive them of their rights, deny them. Pretend they haven't got any. Then they don't know about sunshine or rain either. . . . A millions years accumulating and we know no better than to kick it in the teeth. Now I can't even sense rain although it is there. (139)

Helen is the focal point of the novel. Her intense mental involvement and growth constitute the psychological action of the novel. Bashiam's accident has left him with a clear understanding of his situation. He convinces Helen that their relationship cannot be the same any more; there are greater obligations and responsibilities. "There are some things which one has to do." In this short dialogue Markandaya voices a sense of the inevitability of a return to traditional moorings and to a sense of responsibility with a fuller understanding. Helen echoes Bashiam, "There is something which one has to do." (203) These things enlarge into the unseen responsibilities one has in a community. In fact, Helen is an exploring racial symbol who wants to communicate with another race. Consequently, she makes expedition to the houses of the natives which gladden her heart. Bashiam, the hill man and an educated tribal, becomes her message and medium. Helen's friendship with the native teaches her gleams of truth, nebulous understanding! She learns that sheer dynamism of action alone is not the only means to an end. There are greater values of acceptance, of sympathy. In the silent wisdom of the headman, in the self-contained strength of Bashiam, in the suffering of hill folks, she finds the force of passive resistance. Through her relationship with Bashiam, she tries to fulfill herself. It is the reunion of mind rather than of bodies, of cross culture human affinities rather than promiscuous sexuality. The psychological frigidity of Helen when Clinton makes love to her clearly contrasts with the mental fulfillment she experiences in her union with Bashiam. For the first time in her life she feels a sense of belongingness and develops the sense of inclusiveness: "I belong—I'm not alone. Everything is a part of me, and I'm a part of everything—not just a pop-up cardboard figure." (139)

In her fulfillment, Helen acquires a greater dimension. Apart from being a link between two races, Helen also becomes a symbol of a human being in search of true fulfillment. The development from communication to fulfillment makes her character greater and nobler. She becomes a symbol of universal consciousness. The Western culture, the culture of dams, denies essential human emotions. It atrophies the sustaining springs of human values. In her longing for fulfillment, she is giving a voice to the cry of English culture for the fullness of life. In her relationship with Bashiam, she fulfils all these tenets of human potential. But her relationship with Bashiam cannot be permanent. The novelist gives an allegorical dimension to the conclusion of the novel. The ridges become clear as predicted by the tribal chief. The ridges vindicate clear vision of Helen:

> 'The ridges are clear,' she said. 'Are you sure? He asked, doubtfully, squinting into distance, where the peaks still seemed to him to be tangled with sky, so accustomed had he grown to this persistent view. 'Quite whole and being able to rest upon it.' (221)

Finally, the relationship between Helen and Bashiam comes to an end. The cardinal message of the novel is that all theories of individualism, materialism, rationalism and technology rising from the West cannot be successful unless the Eastern gifts of human values are preserved and forged into them. Human sensibility is more important than technological spirit and the East and the West have not yet been able to merge. They are still alienated because the West has still to imbibe humanism from the East.

The Nowhere Man, as the title of the novel itself suggests, is a magnificent novel of Kamala Markandaya that explores the theme of human loneliness resulting from racial prejudice and immigration. Cultural dualism extends in this novel to a metaphysical condition of isolation. This novel shows in the most palpable form how the novelist is abreast with contemporary sensibility. In its essential spirit, contemporary Western fiction is an existential fable on the human predicament of alienation. The whole range of literature from Eliot to Cocteau, Mann to Sartre, Hemingway to Graham Greene, in one way or the other, is concerned with reshaping the disfigured faces of modern man, man lost *en route*, in search of his identity, his true self. Indian English fiction has also made full cognizance of the changing facets of Indian life and has narratives exploring the dilemma of modern man, his existential problems, his malady of incommunication. Margaret P. Joseph rightly puts it: "In this novel, Markandaya has presented a vision of East-West Encounter in the specific milieu of Indo-British relationship in a country of chequered history."[2]

Half a century back, Rudyard Kipling who was born in India and was a Nobel Prize winner also put his world vision in the oft quoted line: 'East is East, and West is West,/ Never the twain shall meet.' Kipling's account of Indo-British relations is quite objective and balanced. The British ruler went to one extreme by luxurious deeds of building rails and roads and bridges while they went to another extreme by oppressing the Indian in various ways and behaving with them brutally. The hero of this novel is Srinivas who falls a victim to this dilemma.

In *The Nowhere Man*, Kamala Markandaya deals with this contemporary dilemma of man with insight and understanding. The narrative technique, the connotative power of language, the imagery and configuration of emotional situations—all these help to form a sort of fictional ideogram of human isolation.

Disinheritance and rootlessness form the crux of human predicament in the contemporary world. A renaissance man like Marlow's Dr. Faustus could talk of the topless tower of Ilium and express his desire to become immortal with a kiss. John Donne has pronounced: 'No man is an Island;/ Every man is a part of the continent, every man is an island unto himself.' He is alone in the crowd. Instead of a Dr. Faustus or a Tamburlaine, a King Lear or a Macbeth, one finds 'a patient etherized upon a table,' a hollow man, a Prufrock, a Blanche De Bois retreating to the mental asylum or a Vladimir or Estragon waiting for Godot or a Willy Loman broken and torn by values that he has pursued all his life. Feelings of loneliness, anguish, alienation and futility have made terrifyingly deep roots into the Western life. The protagonist of Dostoevski is 'possessed,' Camus' is 'outsider,' Kafka's is under the 'trial,' Beckett's is 'absurd,' Bellow's is 'displaced,' and Ellison's is 'invisible.' These tormented individuals are symptomatic of the disinheritance of the Western life. Luckily the experience of disinheritance and futility has not percolated in the wide fabric of our Indian life in its entirety but it has decidedly pierced into the life of a significant segment of our society. Life in India is also no longer poised, tranquil and composite. Life in our country too is changing fast and its changing facets are forcefully brought out in Indian English novels. Kamala Markandaya, Nayantara Sahgal, Anita Desai and Arun Joshi have given a fictional form to this new experience of the emerging dilemma of human loneliness. Rootlessness and ardent sense of quest for one's identity are the *leit motif* of the Western fiction of Kafka, Sartre, Camus, Mann, Durrell, Saul Bellow and Malamud. Their protagonists grope in the labyrinths of existence; their dilemma is metaphysical. They are living metaphors of loneliness.

Kamala Markandaya's *The Nowhere Man* is a novel written on the theme of immigration finally sublimating into the metaphysical dilemma of human isolation. The root of the problem lies deep in cultural displacement.

The novel tells the story of a south Indian Brahmin, named Srinivas, who after much toil settles in London, under compelling circumstances. Srinivas hails from Madras, comes of a respectable and well-to-do family and is considerably intelligent and promising right from the very beginning of his academic career. It is pointed out that he got distinction in Intermediate and the Vice-Chancellor, Mr. Drinkwater, an English man, conferred upon him a medal for his spectacular achievement. Narayan, Srinivas' father, is ambitious in his plans. Around the First World War, i.e. 1914 to 1918, a great political upheaval took place in the world, making the future of man dark and dismal. It was now difficult to predict the future of nations. Just at that time, Mahatma Gandhi was emerging as a harbinger of peace and humanity. He was experimenting with truth in his own way and launched his freedom movement through twin means of 'Ahinsa' and 'Satyagrah.' Inspired by a lawyer neighbour, Srinivas gets involved in freedom movement. Srinivas is wedded to Vasantha, a girl of the lawyer's family. Vasantha's brother Vasudev, inebriated by a passion to lay down his life at the altar of the motherland throws himself into national movement and distinguishes himself as an ardent freedom fighter. Narayan makes a significant gesture by giving up the traditional dress and putting on 'Khadi' as advised by Mahatma Gandhi.

The story takes a sudden turn when the Governor comes on a visit to the college. The hall is packed with Indians; British people are few in number. The Deputy Principal of the College, Plat, offers bitter comments on the shabby dress of Narayan and Srinivas. The Governor wants the British Anthem to be sung on the occasion. This is revolting to the ego of the father and the son. Narayan mutters the Indian National anthem in almost audible voice. This is sufficient to incur the displeasure of the foreigners. Narayan, thereafter, finding no way out, babbles and shockingly enough is declared a lunatic by the British official and is soon sent to a mental asylum. He has been serving in a government college in Madras. The story graphically tells us how Narayan who was bullied by the British officials was subjected to untold humiliation, insult and inhuman treatment, and how even a junior was made a senior to him in service. All this happened because Narayan was an Indian. Srinivas moves to London, by the grace of the Deputy Principal. Vasantha joins him in London. Slowly and gradually, their connections with India are severed. Vasantha, however, sticks to her Indian way of living, eating, dressing and thinking. She is in need of stability in life and with this point in view, she persuades her husband to acquire a house in London. She plans for the future of her sons Laxman and Seshu. While Srinivas thinks that acquisition of wealth and property might encumber them, 'shackle them to brick and mortar' and block their return to India once for all; Vasantha, though truly Indian, is pragmatic and worldly wise in her approach and persuades Srinivas to acquire a house. She never thinks herself to be a Londoner. Nostalgic feeling is always dominant in her. In fact she considers herself superior to the white people as she belongs to a religion of cosmic concepts dealing with high values of life in contrast to the parochial as well as ephemeral Christianity which she describes a religion not as old as Hinduism. It hardly dates back to ten years. Vasantha has a sense of pride when she acquires a house: "At last we have achieved something. A place of our own where we can live according to our likes although in alien surroundings: and our children after us, and after them theirs."[3]

Though Srinivas has acquired property, his family has not been accepted by the whites and they are known as the people at No. 5. In fact, they have made an island India on the British soil. But the sons Laxman and Seshu are different. Brought up in Christian environment and educated in Christian school, they do not inherit any Indian trait. They are examples of the second generation of immigrants who are neither here nor there. Their alienation is complete because their roots are completely cut off and their connection with the adopted environment is tenuous. Seshu seems to have some feelings for his parents and had he remained alive, he could have been reclaimed. Laxman is almost an alien and he deems himself to be a part of the English landscape. His feet are tied fast to the British soil. When the woman offers a suggestion: "Go back where you belong," Laxman emphatically replies "I belong right here." (261) This is enough to show the operation of his mind and his mode of thinking. In fact, Laxman has tried to identify himself with English culture and British way of life. He is a pillar of the community, employer of thousands, a magistrate and member of the hospital management committee. The question of 'them and 'us' raised by the racists disturb him to the marrow of his bones and he broods over his situation:

> Whatever anyone might say or think, he knew he belonged, and where belonged. To the country in which he was born and lived and labored, not in some reservation bustled up within it. Whatever fathers of sons or sons of bitches might think suitable inmate for ghetto he was not, and did not intend to be. (271)

The family falls into shambles with the advent of war. Laxman and Seshu work in the army. Seshu's sentimentality gets him discharged from the army. He begins to work as an ambulance driver and while discharging his duties, he dies in an accident. Laxman, after a meritorious war service, marries an English girl and settles down at Plymouth as a business man. Vasantha has planned for her sons and has named her house as 'Chandraprasad.' But to her great shock, she dismally fails to select the bride for her son. Her heart is further broken when she is not invited to come to her son's place at Plymouth. She has some sentiments left in her heart and she has demarcated the rules of the house for the wife and children of her sons. But the irony of the situation becomes conspicuous when Laxman writes on the occasion of the birth of the baby that they need not come up as his in-laws are still staying there and in addition there is only one spare bed room. Vasantha's heart sinks in despair. The novelist presents this heart-rending scene in a highly moving manner:

> 'What does that matter?' asked Vasantha, bewildered. 'Is a room essential? I would have slept anywhere. In a corridor or the kitchen.

> Just to see the baby.' 'They don't do things like that in this country,' said Srinivas, 'A dozen people, sleeping in one basement, during the war,' she reminded him, 'The war is over,' he said. (35)

In the absence of the expected reunion of the family, Vasantha collapses and dies leaving Srinivas all alone, desolate and depressed in the big house and the world. Two deaths, of his younger son Seshu and of his wife, make him a broken reed. The callousness of Laxman, his only living son, intensifies his grief and isolation further. He goes to the river Thames to pour the ashes of his wife. He sprinkles Ganges water on the ashes of his wife and puts them into the currents of the river Thames. At this moment, he feels in his breath and bones the identity of Vasantha, who remained wholly Indian. The description is reminiscent of Rupert Brooks' famous poem 'The Soldier' in which the poet describes strong patriotic feelings of the British soldier. Fighting on the soil of France, the British soldier is so rooted to his soil that he considers every corner of the foreign field, where his dead body will be buried, a part of England:

> If I should die, think only this of me:
> That there's some corner of foreign field,
> That is for ever England

Vasantha's position is no different from that of the aforementioned British soldier. Although she spends a large part of her life in England and also breathes her last in England, she does not merge her identity in England. She is exclusively Indian throughout.

Srinivas' life is a life of alienation and misery. He is living desolately. One day he comes across Mrs. Pickering, a very poor old divorcee and a former nurse. The meeting of Srinivas with Mrs. Pickering is a significant incident in the novel. It turns a new leaf in the life of Srinivas. Their meeting and then their gradual intimacy are most natural and needed by the situation. Soon after the demise of Vasantha, Srinivas falls ill. His protracted illness makes him sentimentally weak. Dr. Radcliffe is called in. He finds Mrs. Pickering by the side of ailing Srinivas. Besides being a doctor, Dr. Radcliffe is a friend of Srinivas. The doctor suspects that Mrs. Pickering might be Srinivas' wife. But Mrs. Pickering tells in clear terms, "I'm not his legal wife." (160) Srinivas laughs out the problem passing a general remark that Mrs. Picketing is common law spouse. As the story advances it becomes clear that there is no sexual relation between Srinivas and Mrs. Pickering. They no doubt live together under the same roof but each look upon the other as essential company. They carry the burden of time rather jointly. During one of the visits to his father, Laxman comes to know the presence of Mrs. Pickering. At first he suspects the relationship. But when he meets Mrs. Pickering, he cannot help appreciating her essential goodness.

Srinivas has been neglecting his business and consequently his income dwindles. He rejects the offer of his friend, Abdul, to join his restaurant business. With the passing of time, Srinivas becomes more and more critical of the material comforts. But he has to maintain himself and Mrs. Pickering. The post-war Britain was inflicted with problems of housing and employment. Mrs. Pickering finds an opportunity to earn some money through converting some of the rooms into cheap flats and letting them out to the poor. The house which was acquired for the children of Srinivas is now occupied by the poor people. The dreams of an Indian couple have floundered on the rocks of the British culture. Srinivas withdraws himself into the attic leaving Mrs. Pickering on the ground floor. An old Negro trump occupies the basement. The isolation of Srinivas gets more intense and gradually he insulates himself against the outer world. Subsequently he comes to discover that he is suffering from leprosy. This almost incurable disease is a symbol of complete insularity of man from the society. Leprosy here is both physical and psychic condition.

Srinivas' relationship with his neighbours has not been very congenial and intimate. But he is not responsible for it. The neighbours Mrs. Field and Mrs. Glass have never accepted an Indian family entrenching itself comfortably in their locality while they have been living an economically precarious life. But for a short term during the war, people had forgotten petty animosity and had become a unified community:

> During the war it was like one big family. It seemed to draw every one closer. My wife, you know, she did not mix easily, we did not have many friends . . . but when we were all sheltering in the base-

> ment, the four of us and half the neighbourhood as well, it was quite different. (66)

But when the war is over, two communities fall apart. Old prejudices and hatred begin to leap up flames of violence. Srinivas has never caused any problem. He has always been considerate to his neighbours. Still they have been nourishing ill-will and hatred towards him and his family. Mrs. Field has a Christian conscience. At times, she recognized the essential goodness of Srinivas, when Mr. Field dies, Srinivas and Mrs. Pickering very often call on Mrs. Field to give her solace. They comfort her by their presence at a time when she feels lonely and needs affection. Fred, the son of Mrs. Field, is wayward. He is a menace because of his unwanted aggressiveness and motiveless militancy towards Srinivas. Fred is a worthless young boy who runs away to Australia. But there he is unable to make himself happy. He comes back and finds that a large number of African and Asian immigrants have blocked the way of the sons of the soil to economic security. He attributes this condition of the unemployed English youth to people like Srinivas and becomes the champion of the cause of English youth launching a relentless tyranny against the immigrants. He wants the foreigners to go back. Fred remarks:

> "You got no right to be living in this country," he said and thrust his face close to the brown man's. Berry fumes rose from his nostrils. Srinivas stepped back fastidiously. "Why not?" he asked. "You, telling me you're English?" asked Fred, "By adoption" said Srinivas happily. (164-65)

The passive resistance of Srinivas despite all provocations and in the teeth of all opposition further aggravates the wrath of Fred. Srinivas shows the typical Gandhian element in him when one day Fred and his friends assault him. Mrs. Field cannot understand the hostility of Fred towards the harmless Srinivas. She resents the behaviour of her son. One day when Fred attacks Srinivas, Mrs. Field finds the latter lying on the ground. She feels guilty. She is sure that Fred has done it and, therefore, she asks Srinivas directly if Fred has assaulted him. Srinivas replies in negative. But even this noble gesture hardly creates any effect on the criminal mind of Fred. He plans to burn Srinivas' building. In the meantime Srinivas has served the notice on his tenants that they should vacate the house. He has done this because he is afraid that his tenants might catch infection of the contagious disease he is suffering from. Fred gets a good pretext. He goes on with his machination. He gets all the material ready and enters the basement in the darkness of night. He sets up the machinery. His mischievous operation is being closely watched by the Negro tram. In the darkness as Fred moves about fixing the fuse, the cross belt of his coat is caught in the plumbing of an old disused boiler. As he tries to free himself, he gets firmly held by it. Now the fire spreads all around. Fred groans and cries. But he is engulfed by the fire. He is burnt alive. Srinivas also fights against the fire. He has been caught in the conflagration. People in the neighbourhood, Constable Kent, Laxman, Dr. Radcliffe and Abdul make frantic efforts to get to Srinivas. Laxman rushes into the building and picks up the body of his father. Srinivas opens his eyes, looks around, recognizes Kent and closes his eyes. Dr. Radcliffe declares him dead.

Fred has a scheming mind. He is the disdainful villain of the story. He cannot tolerate the prosperity of others. The poetic justice comes in a glaring manner when evil stands in direct opposition to good. Fred tries to destroy Srinivas. Evil tries to destroy what is good. In an attempt to do so, evil destroys itself.

The story of the novel is a web of complex incidents. It is spun out with the fabric of human relationships. Characters belonging to different cultures and races are brought into the cross-current. It is the story of the brown Indian living amidst the white English. There is the consuming fire of hatred between the races. The death of Fred shows that the hater is invariably destroyed by nature. Kamala Markandaya unquestionably tries to push the situation of racial misunderstanding to serious human conflict. The fact remains that multiple races cannot possibly absorb themselves nor can the diverse cultures assimilate. This dilemma is brought home by the novelist through the medium of a story, the focal point of which is cultural conflict. Margaret P. Joseph aptly observes: "*The Nowhere Man* comes closest of all Kamala Markandaya's books to being a true tragedy. The action is serious and of sufficient magnitude, since it concerns whole races. . . . The incidents arouse not only our pity for the individuals involved, but one fears for the whole human race which permits stances that result in such catastrophes."[25]

One may or may not take this novel as a tragedy. But no one will dispute that here we have spectacle of human conflict, a dilemma that inflicts the whole living human community. Mr. Srinivas is a large-hearted, broad-minded, man of charitable temper. "He is a Christ-like symbol whose Hinduism is not parochial like that of the religion of the British. He does not subscribe to the ethos of girds which is laid upon natural patterns. . . . White man . . . and other men." When Fred dips him in tar, Fred's mother says, "The smell of tar is on you, and the blood of the lamb." (248) This reminds us of the crucifixion of Jesus Christ. The situation assumes a human level that contains both metaphorical and spiritual dimensions.

The true meaning of the novel explicates itself more brightly and cogently if one explores the relationship between Srinivas and Mrs. Pickering cautiously. Like the relationship between Richard and Mira in *Some Inner Fury*, Helen and Bashiam in *The Coffer Dams*, the relationship between Srinivas and Pickering has all human potential. They form a bridge of human understanding. Two desolate derelicts sustain each other:

> They had been derelict in a way, when they met. . . . They had come together, and in the process had solved and restored each other. But it was a muted process, more an easing of aches than violent build up of pleasures, which did not demand the constant stimulus of touch and presence of young love. Even when they lay together it was with a degree of serenity, looking on, as it were, on something which had once been wet and mild, but now was calm. (70)

They are able to see life more positively and with better comprehension. Both of them are symbols of their own cultures and they represent the best, the purified essential spirit of their respective cultures. When Srinivas feels disturbed and vacillates that he is an alien, Mrs. Pickering encourages him and helps him regain his confidence. During the later phase of life when Srinivas is almost a victim to the tyranny of racial hatred, it is Mrs. Pickering's company that nourishes him and helps him gain the power of detachment:

> At home, in Mrs. Pickering's company, was one thing. When he went out it was totally another. Walking through the streets, as he had to, wandering in them as from time to time he felt compelled, a new feeling joined the frailty that could make him cower, walk bent, a man on sufferance apologizing for his presence, like a convict on parole but denied his belligerence. The new feeling was detachment. (172)

Mrs. Pickering not only understands Srinivas, she also cares for him and in her care and concern for the ailing alien abandoned by his son, she embodies the best of the English culture. When Srinivas dies, Mrs. Glass a neighbour of Mrs. Pickering while consoling asks her not to take the event too hard. Mrs. Pickering, in the spirit of a true Christian, sharply reacts to this rather silly remark passed by Mrs. Glass and says that she had helped and nursed the deceased to the best of her capacity. So there is no question of taking the death of Srinivas too seriously. Life is short. We have to live for a few days. Death matters to those who die, neglected and uncared. It is the service of humanity which matters most. Mrs. Pickering is satisfied that she has done her job.

Just as Mrs. Pickering is the symbol of Christian race and culture, Srinivas is also true and authentic symbol of Hindu culture. He is always inclined to help the poor and the depressed. He gives shelter to Mrs. Pickering. He liberally gives the apartments of his house to his tenants on moderate rent. In this, he clings to what may be called Ashram dharma.

His only son Laxman goes away from him and then he and his wife Vasantha start living Vanprastha life. The Hindu concept of life is essentially idealistic. It is divided into four ashramas. It begins with Brahmacharya which is the period of adolescence. In this period a man strictly adheres to the principles of purity, austerity and rigorous discipline and devotes all his time to reading and rendering service to his Guru. This is followed by Grihastha Ashram which begins when a man attains full maturity. It is in this Ashram, when he is permitted to marry and beget children and indulge in worldly activities. The third Ashram is Vanprastha, when the heart of a man is so enlarged that he looks upon everybody as a member of his family. This Ashram needs philanthropic attitude to the world—Vasudhaiva kutumbakam—the whole world is my family. The last one is Sanyas Ashram, when a man renounces the whole world and passes the rest of his life in forest in meditation and quest of God. The way in which Srinivas and Vasantha do service to humanity, help the poor without hoping to get the return, they embrace the diseased and the helpless make them true Vanprastha. Srinivas reaches a stage when nothing disgusts him and no work is mean to him. He looks upon the hatred of Fred and the warmth of his neighbours alike. He, in a way, becomes Sthitapragna, meaning, one whose mind is tranquil. He shows what the *Gita* points out as the highest mark of human perfection—well being to all—*sarve bhavanti sukhinah.* He purifies himself through suffering. He passes through the ordeal of fire but comes out unscathed because he does not die of burns. Later he dies of heart attack. He dies calmly as if he were folding himself. He is not afraid of death. He accepts it as a necessary corollary of life. In achieving the state of detachment and mental poise, he embodies the essence of Indian culture.

Both Srinivas and Mrs. Pickering are metaphors of their cultures interacting with each other in the most human and intimate terms. In them and in their relationship, the East and the West seem to meet and merge. But this relationship cannot endure permanently. The message of the novelist is that the East and the West have begun to understand each other, have started probing into each other's heart. But the novelist is sceptical about their final fusion and adjustment. The story of the novel makes it clear that despite all assimilation and synthesization, the co-existence of the two cultures is an impossibility. The gulf between them is impassable.

This situation of coming closer and yet living part creates the identity of crisis. *The Nowhere Man* is, therefore, the most equivocative in its theme and it is a congruent exploration of Kamala Markandaya into the dilemma of identity. The story of Srinivas is a tragedy of an Indian living in England who tries to assimilate himself into the fabric of British culture but despite his ideals of world citizenship and humanism, he finds himself a nowhere man.

Srinivas passes nearly two third of his life in England and tries to look upon England as his own country. He tells Mrs. Pickering with pride that England is his own country: "My country. . . . I feel at home in it more so than I would in my own." (58)

His friend Abdul of Zanzibari is more pragmatic in his outlook and can see that the British have definite prejudices against Indians and that Indians have to face discrimination all around in pubs, restaurants and customs. He has seen people looking up and down at him and casting cold and callous looks. He remarks:

> I will. I'll tell you what they're saying, right now, this very minute. That black ape, they're saying, meaning me, what's he doing over here in his overheated automobile. Living off our white girls, that's what, stands to reason he must be, else how it happens he can run a motor-car two blocks wide which we can't afford to do? (75)

Abdul advises Srinivas not to think of England as his own country because the British would not allow him to be a part of their culture. "First thing that goes wrong it will be their country, and you go back, nigger, to yours, back where you came from." (75) Srinivas does not agree. However, Srinivas begins to see the reality when the young men of England like Fred, Mike, Joe and Bill under the economic pressure begin to look on the Indians and other immigrants as their enemies, as the source of their problem. The day Fred learns from a mate of his that "The Blacks were responsible. They came in hordes, occupied all the houses, filled up the hospital bed and their offsprings took all the places in schools" (169), he starts behaving fanatically as if he were possessed by the demon of racism. He challenges a coal black man with thick lips sweeping the streets: "Here, you, you got no right to be in this country. You bugger off, see." (289) Fred teases and harasses Srinivas and forces him to realise that he has no right to live in England. In fact, under the consuming fire of racism, Fred has begun to enact the role of a leader of the white race.

> Fred felt, he was born to lead, he knew with utter conviction. So he would. He would lead his country men in the fight to overthrow, the evil, hidden forces that were threatening them in their homeland. (168)

Again and again, it is made clear that the racial rancour goes on mounting and a time comes when Srinivas becomes fully alive to the fact that he cannot be a part of the soil of England. If he thinks himself to be so, it is his disillusionment. The incidents which occur in his life one after another make him realize that he has been living in a fool's paradise. Now Srinivas begins to realise the stark truth. He finds himself an unwanted man and tells Mrs. Pickering, "It is time when one is made to feel unwanted, and liable, as a leper, to be ostracized further perhaps beyond the limit one can reasonably accept one self." (193) He gets almost baffled when he realizes that he has no place to go if he leaves England. If at all he ventures to do so, he would be "a nowhere man looking for a nowhere city." (166) The sympathetic words of Mrs. Fletcher, the mother of Fred, reassure him temporarily. Thereupon, Srinivas decides to stay on in England: "I won't. I do belong here now. It was good of you to remind me." (167) But soon afterwards the sense of existential loneliness and the lack of belongingness impinge upon him. He bursts out in sheer frustration. "I have been transformed into a stranger." (230) Srinivas is full of self-analysis:

> For what, at the end of these assimilating years, can the terminal product be said to be? Srinivas asked himself and rose from the bed of teak to view from his window the human congress that denied him. An alien, he replied, speaking for them, in the voice that—if somehow suddenly, he were to be capitulated among them now—they would use. An alien, whose manners, accent, voice, syntax, bones, build, way of life—all of him—shrieked, alien. (230)

In fact, the novel *The Nowhere Man* is an ideogram of isolation and Srinivas is a symbol of quest for identity. He is very much like the hero of Ralph Ellison's novel *The Invisible Man*. *The Invisible Man* treats the racial milieu on the symbolic level, giving it a mythic character and a universal meaning. It is the story of a Negro in which myth submerges in invisibility. The novel is concerned with the identity of a black individual who suffers a painful alienation of individuality. The hero of *The Invisible Man* is a Negro, that of *The Nowhere Man* an Indian. Both are historically uprooted, psychologically alienated and socially segregated. They struggle and stagger, fall and bleed, suffer and grieve. And yet their humanism grants them tragic stature. The suffering of a great man always evokes our pity.

The crisis of identity, which is the predicament of Srinivas, also invites comparison with the heroes of Achebe's *No Longer at Ease*, Naipaul's *A House for Mr. Biswas* and Anita Desai's *Bye-Bye Blackbird*. All these novels explore the experiences of the principal characters who are aliens in their contexts. All these novels depict the tragic world and explore how an individual is powerless before the inexorable demands of the world around him. *No Longer at Ease* tells us the story of a young man, Obion Kan Kua, who returns to Nigeria after studying for four years in the University of England. The double consciousness of the colonial situation or the dualism of culture is the central point in the novel. The novel begins with the trial of Obi who is charged with corruption. Obi apparently betrays the trust that Mafia progressive union has put on him. *No Longer at Ease* is, in fact, not so much about Obi's crime as about its motive. It does not so much tell a story as project a vision.

In V.S. Naipaul's *A House for Mr. Biswas,* we find a fuller and more exhaustive symbol of exile and rootlessness. The novel begins with Mohan Biswas, a sacked journalist, dying at the age of forty-six in his mortgaged house in Sikkim Street of Spain. He is a man without money, suffering from illness and despair. He has his wife and four children. And yet he is struck again and again by the wonder of being alone in his own house.

Anita Desai's *Bye-Bye Blackbird* also describes the story of an Indian immigrant in England. It covers various dimensions of cultural clash between the British and Asiatic. One such clash is the relationship of marriage between the members of two groups. Adit Sen, a young man from India, lives in England with his English wife Sarah, unable to find a decent job in India in spite of a degree from British University. Adit Sen returns to England and settles down there. With some difficulty, he is able to find a job of travel agent. Fed on English literature and exposed directly to English life and manner, he develops a sense of cultural affinity with England. Like Srinivas, he tries to assimilate himself into the adopted culture. But his fate is no different from that of Srinivas. Like

Srinivas, he too fails to adjust himself in alien environment.

Chinua Achebe's hero Okonkwo presents a contrast to Srinivas. His people have been ill-treated by the whites. But far from being passive like Srinivas, he lies sleepless on his bamboo bed, planning revenge. When the white men's messenger breaks up a meeting, he kills the leader. But he senses the fact that his co-villagers will not support him in his rebellion. So he escapes stealthily, hangs himself, filled with despair at the falling apart of his countrymen under the influence of the white intruders. Unlike Okonkwo, Srinivas is incapable of killing anyone. Unlike him, he dies 'content,' taking on himself the coloured man's burden in a white society. Srinivas's death may be called martyrdom by some, but some others, like Fred and his friends, may call it ordinary liquidation.

The theme of alienation resulting from withdrawal from one's own cultural setting has been a favourable one to many Hindi novelists although this theme is treated differently by them. Chatursen Shastri's novel, *Kitne Chaurahe* is an instance. In this novel we come across a story in which persons belonging to the same family are wedded with girls of different communities. The experiment does not prove fruitful. Each member of the family is uprooted from the family. The cumulative effect is complete alienation and loneliness in their life. They probably do so with a view to achieve a higher end, i.e. national integration, but on the contrary they miserably fail. They fall a prey to inner conflict, chaos and abandonment.

Srinivas realises he is a nowhere man and that things are not as he believes them to be. Evil exists, in the shape of the forces represented by Fred. Srinivas contributes his share of error to the final tragedy for he makes mistakes. But in his catastrophe, we admire the moral stature of his character. We experience anguish over the waste of human goodness in his tragic death. We do not regret the death of a devil. It is the torture, the anguish, the suffering of a noble man which invariably evokes our sympathy and pity. As in Hardy's novels, we find in this novel a chorus in the neighbours such as Mrs. Fletcher. Mrs. Glass and the men in the pub. Srinivas is literally the scapegoat, bearing on his shoulders the sin of being coloured in a white country, seeming to atone for the crime of existence itself.

Mrs. Pickering helps maintain the balance of Srinivas' mind, though he begins to feel defensive and apologetic about his presence in London. This is followed by detachment: not, the detachment he had learnt in India during the time he was made to suffer by the English. There is much of the Gandhian in him. Even the manner in which he dies invites comparison with Gandhi's assassination. Vimala Rao rightly compares Srinivas and his wife to the old couple in Auden's poem "Refugee Blues" who are reduced to a "Nowhere Couple." The experience of incommunication remains the *raison de ètre* of *The Nowhere Man.*

NOTES

1. Kamala Markandaya, *The Coffer Dams*.(Hind Pocket Books, Delhi), p. 36.
2. Margaret P. Joseph, Kamala Markandaya (Arnold Heinemann, New Delhi, 1980), p. 32.
3. Kamala Markandaya, *The Nowhere Man* (Orient Longman, Delhi 1972), p. 20.

Tension in Togetherness Anita Desai's *Cry, the Peacock* and *Where Shall We Go This Summer?*

> Yes, I cried, yes, it is his hardness—no, no, not hardness but the distance he coldly keeps from me. His coldness, his coldness. And incessant talk of cups of tea and philosophy in order not to hear me talk and, talking, reveal myself. It is that—my loneliness in this house.[1]

Incommunication is a distinctively modern human predicament. In the modern wasteland, human beings fall apart. John Donne had a unifying vision when he said that 'no man is an island/ every man is a part of the continent.' Today, in the western world every man is an island unto himself, caged in his own cocoon. Channels of communication have dried up and human life has become an extended exile. Incommunication emerges from multiple causes; one of the prevailing situations that have led to tension in togetherness is the expanding lack of understanding between man and woman. Anita Desai, the eclectic feminine sensibility of contemporary Indian fiction, has explored this crisis in novel after novel and has carved out wonderful novels. *Cry, the Peacock*, her first novel and *Where Shall We Go This Summer?*, her fifth, have been forged in the smithy of this tension in togetherness.

Anita Desai's *Cry, the Peacock* is an extremely moving novel with a heart-rending story. The novelist's imaginative grasp of incidents and scenes is everywhere sustained. The story has a human substance and it reveals her skill cultivated more by genius than by practice. Though *Cry, the Peacock* is Desai's maiden attempt, it gives evidence of her maturity as a story-teller and a consummate artist. The novel has been written in a fluent and poetic style reminiscent of the style of Emily Bronte, D.H. Lawrence and Virginia

Woolf. The novel looks like a chiselled piece of marble on which some images have been carefully carved out. The style of the novelist reminds us of the style of the novelists falling under the group 'stream-of-consciousness school.' The effect of the novel is heightened by the manner the story is told. The twin qualities of the novelist are the power to sustain suspense and the power to evoke curiosity. These qualities are found in great novelists only. Meena Belliappa finds in the novel "a remarkable attempt to fuse fantasy with perpetual experience."[2] On the other hand Darshan Singh Maini termed it as a 'poetic novel.'

The scene of the novel is set against the background of Delhi, where Gautama, the principal male character of the novel, practises as a busy lawyer. There are casual references to the circular part of Connaught Circus, Red Fort, Jama Masjid and Birla Temple apart from other references connected with Delhi.

The novel presents the story of Gautama and Maya—an unequal match not only temperamentally but physically also. While Gautama is a middle-aged elderly fellow, Maya is tender, young and ambitious in her plans. Maya is twice thwarted to see the sickly constitution of her husband—first, when Gautama is ready for bath and second when he puts off his neck-tie on coming back from the court. On the first occasion, Maya pities Gautama's 'thinness,' 'anemic' skin and his "cage like ribs." (200) And on the second occasion, she finds him so helpless that she compares him with a Gibbon—a long armed ape: "a Gibbon would be defter." (199) Thus, the seed of conjugal rift is sown in the very beginning of the novel.

It is hinted that Maya is under the domineering influence of her father. She is married to Gautama "a stooped and knowledgeable friend of Maya's father." (40) This is what K.R. Srinivasa Iyengar calls 'father fixation.'[3] Once Maya's father chooses Gautama as her prospective bridegroom, Maya has no option but to accede to his proposal. She, like an obedient daughter, born in a traditional Hindu family, succumbs to the whim of her father knowing that she may have to pay heavily for this mischoice. Maya is not only sensitive but contemplative as well by nature. She is in need of a real life partner who can bestow love upon her and confide in her. She wants the congenial atmosphere of domesticity.

The novel records the recollections and reflections of Maya, whose life is now full of cracks. Maya's haunting memories of the bygone days—mostly unpleasant—are woven into the fabric of this novel. The title of the novel *Cry, the Peacock* is highly suggestive because in the cry of the peacock one gets a queer intermingling of life and death, communion and separation, meeting and parting and above all horror before mating. It is this horror which strikes the keynote to the tragic theme of this novel.

Ironically enough, Maya and Gautama are juxtaposed leading to the intricacies that we find in this novel. There is little in common between the husband and the wife. So there is slender chance of their being happy and satisfied. The couple also differs in ideology. Maya has little schooling. She herself admits, "My education you see was restricted to what could be imparted within the brief confines of a small airless chalky class room far from fashionable school." (199) On the contrary, Gautama is an intellectual, he has a roaring practice as a lawyer, he is always surrounded by clients. And what is more, like the postmaster of Rabindra Nath Tagore's story 'Postmaster,' he lives by philosophy alone. Gautama is worldly wise, has a logical brain and power of reasoning. Reflecting upon his busy schedule, Gautama says: "the work piles up, I haven't closed one case, and the other is already waiting." (173) He quotes the *Gita* very often to console his wife. He wants his wife to perpetuate the philosophy of detachment and non-involvement in life which according to him is the secret of enduring peace. Gautama says: "The *Gita* does not preach involvement in tradition. It preaches—recommends rather—detachment on every count." (17) It is difficult for Maya to agree to the philosophy of detachment and dispassion. Maya wants to live the normal life of a wife. She wants a sweet home, a husband who can love her. She hates Platonic love; she craves for love which is physical. She yearns for the sweet kindly touch of her husband, longs for his continued association. She wants to be one with her husband but the misfortune is that Gautama, partly on account of his busy profession and partly because of his philosophical bent of his mind, fails to understand Maya. Maya resents, "I required his closest understanding" (19) and unluckily this understanding is denied to her. Ever since the day of wedding, the cleavage between the couple grows wider with the passage of time. Maya feels alienated from her surroundings and this feeling becomes so oppressive, so suffocating that she no more remains mentally normal. The icon of a lovable husband crumbles fast, leaving her all alone, alienated and battered. The inner conflict of Maya has been brought out by the novelist in all its shades mostly through her monologues. Maya's self-analysis is scattered over the narrative throughout. She is invariably seen talking to herself. An ever-widening gap, incommunication between the husband and the wife is felt throughout the novel. Maya feels quite lonely in Gautama's house. She says: "there was still space of darkness in between, above and around, and it was that which gave the air such weight. Death lurked in those spaces." (22) The agony of loneliness and the spell of darkness separate both Maya and Gautama.

The distance between Maya and Gautama reminds us of D.H. Lawrence's story 'Odour of Chrysanthemums' where one finds alienation and incommunication between the wife and the husband. Elizabeth Bates always felt alienated from her husband Walter so much so that even after he was dead and she stared at his corpse, he seemed to be a stranger to her. Elizabeth felt that she had never seen her husband. The children were the result of sheer biological need. They fought in the dark and the children were born. Elizabeth's frustration in love entailed her frustration in life. The story gives a picturesque description of the agony of the heroine:

> Life with its smoky burning gone from him had left him appall and utterly alien to her. And she knew what a stranger he was to her. In her womb was ice of fear, because of this separate stranger with whom she had been living as one flesh. Was this what it all meant utter in fact separateness, obscured by heat of living?[4]

There was no flow of sympathy between the husband and the wife. They, no doubt, lived together and produced children but there was only the meeting of their bodies and not their deeper selves. The suffering of Elizabeth provides the substance of the story. The hatred of Elizabeth for her husband is pitted against her husband's complete indifference. Elizabeth pitied her husband. The difference was too much for her: "She knew she had never seen him, he had never seen her." (200)

There was complete lack of understanding between the husband and the wife. This again was the result of real and natural pull between the couple which led to the ultimate catastrophe. The death of Walter is a trope that presages the end of the self-destructive mirror. The alienation of Elizabeth reaches its climax when she begins to tidy up her kitchen and asks the children to drink milk as if nothing had happened. D.H. Lawrence is a psychic mariner and this story is a study of least articulate and more decisive moments of sympathy and antipathy between two opposite forces.

So is the case with Mr. and Mrs. Morel in Lawrence's novel *Sons and Lovers* although compared to Anita Desai's *Cry, the Peacock*, the position is just the reverse here. In *Cry, the Peacock* Gautama is intellectual and Maya is naïve and innocent while in *Sons and Lovers*, Mr. Morel is a miner and Mrs. Morel is a cultivated woman. Mrs. Morel is unhappy and unsatisfied in her marriage. She marries Mr. Morel attracted by his sensual gaiety and vitality. But what is conspicuous is the disparity in education and outlook. This impairs and destroys the understanding between the couple. She feels alienated particularly because her husband fails to understand her. The result is that as her sons grow up, she unconsciously tries to draw them into a love relationship with disastrous effect. The subtlety of Lawrence's insight into the psychology of the emotionally possessive mother is nowhere better shown than in the study of the conflict between Miriam and Mrs. Morel for the soul of the younger son Paul. Mr. and Mrs. Morel live together under the same roof. But they are poles apart emotionally. Mr. Morel never feels that she had a husband at all. The agony of separation and incommunication compel her to divert her attention to her sons where she tries to find what she misses in her husband. Her diversion is a reaction against the coldness of her husband towards her which pricks her day and night.

To a great extent, Maya's alienation is rooted essentially in Gautama's philosophical detachment and his unconcerned behaviour towards the basics in life. In a different situation, Gautama would have proved to be a remarkably successful husband. This was a match between two different temperaments—with not even a single link in their physical and mental outlooks to bring them to a closer tie. As the two have opposite temperaments, they drift apart through the very process of their living together. Had they followed the usual procedure of an ordinary marriage that turns the partners into weary strangers in course of time, there would have been nothing amiss. But a Desai heroine cannot succumb to such circumstances. She tries to preserve the deep torturous love for Gautama with childish pleadings: "Is there nothing, I whispered, is there anything in you that should be touched ever so slightly, if I told you, I live my life for you?" (114)

This involvement in her and the complete lack of it in Gautama is the root cause of the maladjustment that creates the fear complex in Maya. From an ordinary pampered hypersensitive child bride, Maya is transformed within four years of married life into a neurotic, homicidal maniac through the grinding process of mindless compromise with her marriage which was doomed to fail right from the beginning. The drum-beats claim her young life into the twilight hours of insanity and then death.

The cry of the peacock, and at the same time the cry of Maya, frustrate her from within. Similar to the monsoon peacock dancing madly and crying for its lover and bleeding profusely before mating in a frenzy of love, Maya's heart cracks up. The novelist employs flashback technique to narrate the story of Maya. This technique provides the novelist an opportunity to move backward and forward as the occasion warrants. Maya says a lot about her agonies, compulsions, inhibitions and longings. At every stage, she exposes her real self. Nothing drastic happens in this novel except the death of Maya's pet dog Toto in the beginning and the death of Gautama at the end. In fact, Gautama's death is the natural corollary of the chain of circumstances in which he has been put. On the other hand, Maya concedes nothing. Nothing is superimposed from her side. Naïve, weak-nerved and impulsive as she is, every word she utters has a deep layer of meaning.

K.R. Srinivasa Iyengar traces the influence of Virginia Woolf on the language of Anita Desai in the novel *Cry, the Peacock.* He identifies Maya with Mrs. Dalloway of Woolf's *To the Lighthouse* in recapturing the past experiences. One may add that the language and style of Anita Desai not only reminds us of the language and style of Virginia Woolf but the whole range of novelists writing psychological novels. Historically this trend began with Dorothy Richardson and continued with Virginia Woolf through James Joyce. The method adopted by the novelists of this school is that in their novels the incidents are connected only by association rather than by logical sequence. It, however, cannot be denied that the novel, *Cry, the Peacock,* bears the stamp of Virginia Wolf's technique. The purple patches of poetry littered here and there in this novel further remind us of the language and style of Emily Bronte, particularly her novel, *Wuthering Heights*.

Cry, the Peacock is a powerful novel and its story is startlingly refreshing. The story is also steeped in Indian mythology. Maya is shown as terror-stricken from the very beginning. Ever since the day the Albino astrologer made a terrible prophecy that either of the spouse would die after four years of marriage, Maya suffers from death obsession. All the merrymakings, the visits to restaurants and cabaret fail to make her happy. She withers slowly and gradually. There is no redemption of an impending danger. When Maya was unmarried, she was full of hope and aspirations. The prophecy of the astrologer comes as a bolt from the blue. A shudder passes over her soul. This prophecy is made in the presence of Maya's Ayah. The astrologer unhesitatingly declares: "Death to one of you. When you are married—you shall be married young. Death—an early one—by unnatural causes." (31) Maya is scared. She makes up her mind not to marry at all, "I will never marry." (31) Maya's dreams are shattered, her hope is gone. The ominous prophecy of the astrologer, which may be likened to the prophecy of the three witches in Shakespeare's *Macbeth* as K.R. Srinivasa Iyengar puts it, guides and controls Maya's whole life till she turns insane and Gautama passes away. When the astrologer finds that his prophecy has adversely affected the mind of Maya, he consoles her "but in the hands of God—He may guide you on to another path if you pray for it to be so, offer sacrifice in order that it may be so." (31) He also cites the example of Prahlad who was thrown from the mountain, was flung into fire but was saved by Lord Krishna. It is a poor consolation which does not convince Maya. The astrologer described in this novel is not the astrologer of R.K. Narayan's story, 'An Astrologer's Day,' where the astrologer tells everything from personal knowledge. Here the astrologer is a serious man who firmly believes in the constellation of stars. In a dry, trite tone, characteristic of a real astrologer, he warns Maya, "stars do not lie and so it is best to warn you." (29) The astrologers' prophecy which he makes by studying the palms of Maya is reaffirmed by him by an examination of her horoscope and curves and lines on her forehead. It is now the fourth year since she was wedded to Gautama. All these years, Maya has been thinking negatively. Whatever she thinks or acts is the product of her morbid imagination. She feels a sense of complete aloofness. She is fed up of her unusual existence. Her marital life becomes almost a riddle. She cannot persuade herself to adjust herself in the new environment. Gautama is "tied fast to the sordid of this world." He is like Gradgrind of Charles Dickens novel, *Hard Times*, who always cries: "Fact and fact and nothing but fact." This pernicious philosophy is not at all liked by Maya. It does not suit Maya's mind which is initially trained in plain thinking. In a kind of nervous excitement, Maya recollects her past:

> In Gautama's family one did not speak of love, far less of affection. One spoke—they spoke—of discussions in parliament, of cases of bribery and corruption revealed in government, of newspaper editors accused of libel, and the trials that followed, of trade pacts made with countries, made across the sea, of political treaties with those across the mountains, of distant revolutions of rice scarcity and grain harvests. (46)

Maya is not able to decide whether Gautama's mother is favourably or inimically disposed towards her. Once Gautama's mother had remarked to Maya:

> 'It was wise of Gautama to have married you, Maya,' in a voice tinged with harshness, so that I could not tell whether she said this out of affection or had some motive far removed from any personal feeling. (47)

If at all Gautama's mother has some love for Maya, it is for the sake of money only. Maya distinctly remembers her mother-in-law who had once questioned, "When will your father send another cheque, Maya? Tell him I need it urgently—the nurses in the crèche have not been paid this month." (47-48) Maya is fully conscious of the fact, "she was not even one of those human beings whose comfort and health she felt responsible for" (48) it is easy to gather from the story that Gautama's mother has many children. Gautama is the eldest. Others are journalists, teachers and scientists. Two of them are still students.

The novel tells the woeful story of Maya. Gautama has no time to stand and stare. He is in the habit of blowing off the worries of his life through the puff of cigarettes. 'The life saving chain of cigarettes' (150) is sufficient to relax him. Then there is the basic difference between the husband and the wife with regard to attitude to life. Maya thinks that her husband needs nothing in life except money which he considers 'basic' in life. He is little concerned with 'love or life.' His voice is 'invariably reassuring, logical, calm.' Addressing Maya, Gautama remarks, 'Love—the great and splendid ideal of the young ultimately becomes, you will find, for the man, a matter of dealing with the bills that come in, and, for the woman, worrying about them." (14) Maya is even rebuked by Gautama:

> Like most young people, you cannot understand that reality and idealism are one and the same thing. Life is not a matter of distinguishing between the two, but of reconciling them. But, in such matters, we are opsimaths, and one day you shall learn that these ideals eventually resolve themselves into realities one has known all one's life, and spurned perhaps. (20-21)

Gautama lives in his self-made world of ideas and ideals. He thinks that Maya does not know how to live life. He even goes to the length of branding Maya a 'neurotic':

> Neurotic, that's what you are. A spoilt baby, so spoilt she can't bear one adverse word. Every one must bring a present for little Maya—that is what her father taught her. (115)

Gautama is unhappy over the way Maya had been brought up. His angry outburst is revealed when he grumbled over Maya's vain idealism:

> Life is a fairy tale to you still. What have you learnt of the realities? The realities of common human existence, not love and romance, but living and dying and working, all that constitutes life for the ordinary man. You won't find it in your picture books. And that was all you were ever shown—picture-books. What wickedness to raise a child like that! (115)

Gautama further observes that Maya's father is responsible for spoiling her:

> He is the one responsible for this—for making you believe that all that is important in the world is to possess, possess—riches, comforts, posies, dollies, loyal retainers—all the luxuries of the fairy tales you were brought up on. (115)

After Maya is wedded to Gautama, she enters a different world. The aim of human life for the members in Gautama's household is not an epicurean delight in the pleasures of the senses. They are ontologically secure people with a strong internal locus of control. Here frank and objective evaluation of each other does mean the snapping of the bond between the parents and children. Gautama's mother loves children, no doubt, but she does not expect subjugation from them. They suffer from no inhibitions, no anxieties and express themselves without the fear of being misunderstood. This impresses as well as confuses Maya. Her mother-in-law is neither an idealist, nor a perfectionist nor a romantic and yet Maya feels her mother paling into insignificance in front of this small-statured somewhat sloppy woman who is endowed with the "marvellous capacity of indifference to everything that was not vital, immediate and present." (162)

In so far as Maya is concerned, the disintegrated, neurotic and fearful Maya loses control over her environment and fails to relate herself meaningfully to Gautama who every now and then stumbles purely by accident.

Gautama perpetuated Gradgrindian philosophy of 'facts.' When Toto, the pet dog of Maya, is buried, he stoically remarks: "Burial and cremation are facts." (16) He reiterates his philosophy, "Facts that matter." (16) He takes the death of Toto as a hard fact, a fact that cannot be averted. But for Maya the death of Toto is something more than a mere fact. She retorts: "Oh, Gautama, pets mightn't mean anything to you and yet they mean the world to me." (16)

Gautama is worldly-wise. He lives in the world of material things. On the other hand, Maya lives in the world of dreams. This is what makes all the difference between the two.

Gautama is always out to impose his pragmatic views on Maya which is resented by her: "I mean, how you can dictate." But Gautama goes on arguing spirally and elliptically to justify his stand. For him, sticking to tradition is a folly. Toto is dead and gone. Now there is no point in remembering him. People cling to tradition because they want to leave something behind them: "A wealthy Zamindar might introduce novelties into his house, to impress fashionable motor cars. But he will not deviate from tradition when it comes to birth, marriage or death. Oh no. Because he knows, and even the worst fool will accept this truth, by sheer force of persistence, that the only thing that continues to live is tradition. Not every tradition, ancient as it might be—and that is why we always have the antediluvian sector amidst the older generation that spends its time in vociferously mooring bygone way—but those that have certain reasons, and have proved, by time, to be durable. Having endured, they must be worthy of endurance, claim these simple souls, and thus they find something they can dedicate their small silly mind too with impunity." (16-17) Obviously Gautama treats tradition as a part of hypocrisy. He takes pleasure in rebutting the notion of Maya that Toto is worth-remembering. He emphatically says: 'Now what is there in the ancient rites of cremation that is worth-remembering?' (16)

Maya is a simple lady and she is simply dazzled by the arguments of Gautama. Their traumatic differences grow wider with the passage of time. Maya suffers from a sense of complete isolation and ennui.

Maya, however, stands on the opposite pole. She does not like the idealism or philosophy of her husband. She lives in a perpetual state of tension. She even does not like her husband offering her tea. She detests Gautama's coldness and harshness:

> Yes, I cried, yes, it is his hardness—no, no, not hardness, but the distance he coldly keeps from me. His coldness, his coldness, and incessant talk of cups of tea and philosophy in order not to hear me talk and, talking, reveal myself. It is that—my loneliness in this house. (9)

Gautama presents an opal ring to Maya. Maya gladly accepts it. But Maya has grave doubt that the ring has been presented to her by her husband out of sincere love. Gautama simply looks at the costly ring ignoring the skin beneath the ring: "He did not notice translucent skin beneath, the blue flashing veins that ran under and out of the bridge of gold." (9)

Gautama works in his office till late at night. Maya wants to retire to bed early. She needs her husband's company. Gautama asks Maya to go to bed while he is himself drowned in papers:

> Telling me to go to sleep while he worked at his papers, he did not give another thought to me, to either the soft, willing body or the lonely, wanting mind that waited near his bed. (9)

Maya pines endlessly for the love of her husband. Gautama is lost in the vanity fair of life. What a world of difference between the two? It is something like fitting a round peg in a square hole. The distress emerging out of this disparity forms the basic structure of this novel. For Gautama, Maya is a 'pampered' girl. For Maya, Gautama lacks 'closest understanding.' Maya always accuses her husband of not understanding her properly: "You do not understand." (145) Gautama feels that his wife has done him "injustice." (145) Harbans, an old Sikh friend of Gautama from his student days, describes him as "always the brainy type, always studying, always standing first in examination." (74) This cognitive element in Gautama makes him completely unfit as a successful husband.

The novel begins with the curtain rising on the death of Toto, Maya's pet dog. Maya has been emotionally so attached to her pet dog that she cannot bear its death. She wails and moans. At this moment, she longs for the company of her husband who unfortunately is busy in his profession:

> She sat there, sobbing, and waiting for her husband to come home. Now and then she went out on to the verandah, and looked to see if he were coming up the drive which lay shrivelling, melting and then shrivelling again, like molten lead in a grove cut into the earth and out of the corner of her eyes, could not help glancing, as one cannot help a tie, at the small white corpse lying at one end of the lawn, under a sheet, under the limes. (5-6)

Just at that moment a servant arrives and announces the arrival of an advocate much to the dislike of Maya: "'No!' she cried, "and fled to the bedroom to fling herself on to the bed and lie there." (7) She thinks of the "small still body stiffened into the pain-stricken posture at the moment of death, and of the small sharp yelp in the throat as it suddenly contracted." (7)

Thus, at the outset of the novel, the novelist gives an inkling of how there was an impassable gulf between Maya and Gautama, the wife and husband with regard to attitude to life. Maya was impulsive, tender-hearted, susceptible to a tragic incident while Gautama was hard-boiled, without sentiment or sympathy. When Maya is submerged in the thought of the death of her pet dog, Gautama talks of a cup of tea. He is least concerned with the sorrow of his wife. Not to say of sharing the sentiment of his wife, he is a stranger to her. He has nothing to do with the joy or suffering of his wife. This chasm between the couple is difficult to bridge. This is seen at every step in the novel. In such a circumstance, it is but natural that Maya should feel lonely, alienated, isolated and completely cut off.

The first part of the novel ends on this note of suspense on Toto dying. The image of the 'spilt tea' suggests the lurking danger. The second part of the novel deals at length with the malady in the life of Maya. Maya and Gautama are projected against a panorama of follies and vices and superstitions. Maya fairly recollects some of the most unpleasant incidents of the first year of her married life. Maya's father wanted to take her to Darjeeling in summer. Maya, however, wanted her husband, Gautama, to accompany her to Darjeeling. She did not like to leave Gautama behind.

Maya, unable to establish rapport with Gautama, finds her life meaningless. Her loneliness, her aching heart and gradual deterioration of her psyche make her an existentialist character. She admits:

> For there never was a doubt in my mind, now that I remember, as to the definite truth that I did indeed have a place in it. Not only I, but my small dog, whose sad journey I followed with my mind, even as my eye traced pattern after majestic pattern amidst the proud constellations. (26)

"I would go without you? Leaving you behind in the heat?" Gautama had retorted: "I dare say I can manage, considering I did so for a great many years before I married you." Maya says: "Please, don't speak like that" (41). When Maya had expressed her desire to visit south India—Travancore, Cochin, Mysore, and Malabar—to see the Kathakali dances there, Gautama had reacted against this proposal also because it was silly on her part to undertake a journey to south India in the hot season, particularly when the dance party was soon to visit Delhi. And in addition, it would involve much expenditure. It isn't for nothing that Maya says about her husband: "He uses words as pebbles to strike with." (139) This is the beginning of the bickering between the husband and the wife. The death of Toto, Maya's pet dog, brings unusual change in Maya. Death is inevitable. Like Siddhartha Maya always ponders over Death. The ominous shadow of death hovers over her whole life. She always thinks of death, weighs life in terms of death. She considers life meaningless, a passing show. She longs for immortality. Gautama's preaching with regard to the qualities of *Sthita Prajna* as described in the *Gita* fall flat on her ears.

To some extent Gautama may be said to be a sceptic. He finds the philosophy of the *Gita* shaky. He has no belief in its practical utility, at least in the context of his own life:

> That is the end of our philosophical aspirations—to exist like a lily upon water, rooted in water yet with its petals dry, untouched by it.

> The lamp placed in a windless corner, unflickering. The tortoise with its limbs withdrawn from the external world—oh, the entire cult of symbols that we have for this ideal existence. But who is capable of it? I, with my books, my work, or you with your sensual pleasure in living? (119)

Gautama prefers Christ to Buddha because while the former dedicated his life for the well-being of the sufferers, the latter "meditated beneath the bo tree, his eyes closed to death." (119) More than once, he tries to impose his ideas upon Maya. He uses the word 'listen' four times to impress upon Maya that whatever he says is right. But Maya has nothing to do with Gautama's cold philosophy or erudition or his legal acumen. She boldly affirms again and again that she lives for Gautama. But Gautama remains detached from Maya throughout. Seated upon a soft tiger skin, "too fastidious to touch the common earth, with those long, clean-cut hands of his, too fastidious to admit such matters as love, with its accompanying horror of copulation, of physical demands and even, overbearingly, spiritual demands of possession and rights won and established." (113)

It is impossible for Maya to enter the vast world of Gautama. In great frustration and agony, Maya cries:

> In his world there were vast areas in which he would never permit me and he could not understand that I could even wish to enter them, foreign as they were to me. On his part, understanding was scant, love was meagre, not to be loved as one does love. (104)

Maya wants Gautama to explain what love means to him. Gautama philosophizes: "Love? Love that is without any ambition, without any desire, without any life except that which keeps it alive, burning, yes, that is well." (119-20)

Maya cannot conceive of this kind of love, she conceives of love on the earthly plane. This gulf in the modes of life between the husband and wife is seen everywhere. Maya is completely cut off from her husband, if not on the spiritual plane, at least on the material plane. This feeling is so overwhelming, so overpowering that she has no sequence of words to explain her suffering. Maya wants to see her husband as her friend, philosopher and guide. But she finds him a good-for-nothing creature, despite all his scholarship and wisdom:

> You are—untouched. How can I explain it to you then? I shall never be able to tell you now. You shall never help me. It is all true. One of us will win, the other must lose. (114)

Maya is consigned to a world of gloom and oblivion. She feels no charm in this world. She has a husband, no doubt, but he is only for the sake of name. There is no pull of love between the two, no emotional tie. The marriage is a misalliance. Maya describes her predicament in the following words:

> The silence descended upon me again now, and while I held my soul, still burning, in my hands, I saw my body detach itself from it and float away, to rest upon the dim mirror where I could gaze upon it from a cool distance. (105)

Maya develops hatred for herself, she is not sure that her husband likes her:

> One might think it a lovable face. But it was not the face that a man like Gautama could love. He might be charmed by it, momentarily, diverted by it, for a while, but to capture him entirely, if a fleshy face could do it, it would have to be a finer one, the elongated etiolated one of an intellectual, refined by thought and reflection, bereft of the weakness of impulses, aloof from coarseness and freshness. (105)

Thus slowly and gradually unmitigated good dawns upon her:

> I entered a new vista of knowledge. I forced myself into believing that I could see now what must be the reason for my hating it so, for Gautama's spurning it. (106)

Even in respect of the concept of love, Gautama and Maya stand on opposite poles:

> Was it so unforgivable to wish to share in human friendliness? In companionship? To Gautama it was—for a woman, for a light-headed woman, a childish one, like myself. In his world there were vast areas in which he would never permit me, and he could not understand that I could even wish to enter them, foreign as they were to me. On his part, understanding was scant, love was meagre, not to be loved as one does love. (104)

For Gautama, love is meant for the light-hearted woman. It is not meant for a serious and sensible woman. On the contrary, Maya thinks that love is the whole existence of a woman. Addressing Gautama Maya says:

> "You know nothing of me—and of how I can love. How it is important to me." Maya hated Gautama on this score. "You've never loved. And you don't love me. . . . Oh, if you do, if you say you do, it means nothing. Love has no importance for you, it is merely attachment." (112)

Gautama was "too fastidious to touch the common earth" He was "too fastidious to admit such matters as love." And what was more; he cannot face the "horror of copulation." (113)

Gautama and Maya's basically different notions of love separate them. Maya knows that with his cut and dry theory of love, her husband will never love her, not to say of physical communion. Love for him is a trite, commonplace phrase which is reserved for the female folk only.

There was no pull of love between the husband and wife. Maya grieves: "had there been a bond between us, he would have felt its pull, I thought of him so deeply, but, of course, there was none." (108) This reminds us of mechanical life described in *The Waste Land* by T.S. Eliot. Eliot has given a vivid description of the face value of love. The young carbuncular arrives at the female typist in the evening when she has already taken her meals and feels bored and tired. The lover pretends to show amorous gestures. The suggestion is that there is complete collapse of deeper spiritual meaning of love. Love has become a source of titillation or gratification of the senses.[5]

In fact, Gautama does not belong to the world of Maya. Hence, there is no question of conjugal harmony. Her husband's apathy for her eats up the vitals of her soul. Maya gets several proofs of her husband's apathy towards her:

> In a sudden, impulsive longing to be with him, to be close to him, I leapt up, full of decisions to make haste in undressing, preparing myself, then joining him at last; so that we could go out into the garden, together, where the beds had been made for the night and were cooling in the moonlight. But when I went to rouse him from

> the couch, with a touch, I saw that he had closed his eyes not with mere tiredness, but in profound, invulnerable sleep, and was very far from any world of mine. (93)

In such moments Maya felt a complete nervous break-down. She wanted that somebody should come forward to administer morphine so that she might sleep in peace. Gautama thought that Maya was just pretending. He branded her sickness as 'exhibitionalism.' (89) Not only that, he equated her 'exhibitionalism with egoism or megalomania.' (90)

In the second part of the novel, an attempt has been made to explain the implication of the cry of the peacock. Maya knows what is the meaning of the cry of the peacock. The prophecy of the astrologer haunts her mind. The mark on her forehead, Maya believes, is conspicuous enough to spell disaster:

> It must be a mark upon my forehead, which had been so clear to the opaque eye of the albino who had detected it, upon which the stars now hurled themselves vengefully, and which prophesied a relentless and fatal competition between myself and Gautama. (106)

Maya is in confusion as to who, the husband or the wife, would die young unnaturally and violently four years after marriage. Maya tries to give this ominous mark on her forehead a locality. "Was it an arrow? A coffin? A cross? A star? Was it between the eyes? At the temple? Was it dark? Was it pale? (106)

Maya is afraid to see her own face reflected in the mirror. She knows that she has been damned by the albino. It is four years now. The fatal day is fast approaching. Then why use cosmetics? What's the use of vermilion for her? Maya's sombre tone is sufficient testimony to her prolonged suffering:

> I could no longer bear to see that clear ignorant and insane face, and looked away, down at the rows of little gleaming crystal bottles of perfume and *attar*, *sindoor* and *kumkum*. (106)

In a drooping rather hysteric mood, Maya cries violently. "Am I gone insane?" (98) She is in search of a shelter but finds none in this world:

> Father! Brother! Husband! Who is my saviour? I am in need of one. I am dying, I am in love with living. I am in love, and I am dying.

> God, let me sleep, forget, rest. But no, I'll never sleep again. There is no rest any more—only death and waiting? (98)

Maya has a strong will to live. This *Jijisva* does not let her die. The life-instinct is dominant in her.

Gautama and Harbans laugh at Maya because she believes in the prediction of the albino. Gautama disdains to discuss so puerile a subject as astrology. He considers himself above astrology:

> No educated adult can seriously be expected to believe that the patterns or the movements of the astral bodies—solids, after all, of earth and ice and rock—or the lines formed in the palms of your hands, and in those monkeys and gorillas as well, have the remotest influence upon our deeds and actions in our everyday lives—or those of the apes. (79)

Harbans who is himself an amateur palmist claims to convince Maya of the futility of the astrologer's prophecy within five minutes. But both Gautama and Harbans miserably fail to convince Maya. It is difficult for Maya to get rid of the astrologer's prophecy. The astrologer is all pervasive for Maya. She always thinks of "the albino, the magician, his dull, opaque eyes, the hand twitching, and the fold of cloth between the swallowing thighs." (64)

Broken, terror-stricken, almost insane, Maya sees nothing but death in life. She has a friend named Leila. Her husband is dying of tuberculosis. Leila falls in love with him when he is seriously bed-ridden. Like Maya, Leila is also a fatalist. Her tacit admission is: "It was all written in my fate long ago." (39) Leila is to have a baby soon. She goes to Birla Mandir in order to offer prayers to be blessed with a son because she has no male child. Maya pities her condition. The picture of death once again comes in full form before her. Then there is the marital problem of Nila, her husband's sister. Nila wants to sever her relation with her husband. She wants to obtain a decree of divorce from her husband. She seeks Gautama's help in this regard who, of course, shows his inability to help her. While Maya reacts to the sight of Leila's pregnancy particularly when her husband is to die soon, she is in favour of Nila's plan who wants to be separated from her husband .What is the use of living with a husband who cannot put-up with the frailties of his wife, who cannot accommodate and understand her?

Maya's own condition is no better than that of Leila or Nila. Gautama is not able to understand the misery of Maya. Maya's own misery is sufficient to torture her. The problems of Leila and Nila add to her misery. Maya understands that the sole cause of her misery is her unnecessary involvement in the affairs of others. She frankly admits: "There lay the catalysis of my unrest. I had grown too involved." (67)

Gautama is more practical than Maya in this respect. He does not like that his wife should needlessly get involved in other's affairs. Addressing his wife, he says in an ironic tone:

> You are a grown woman now, Maya, no light-headed child. You must not allow yourself to grow so upset about these things. What if they do live in a grubby house? What if she is pregnant again? What if they were so dull? Why should you allow it to affect you in this manner? There is nothing constructive in your misery, after all. Besides, your life is your own, so different from theirs—your world completely separated. Tell me, is any part of your life as drab, or as depressing as theirs? You must not allow yourself to grow so painfully involved. (67)

He even does not hesitate in calling his wife insane for reacting to the pregnancy of Leila.

> If a man were to react to the sight of pregnancy by bursting into tears, Maya, no court of law would consider him sane or sober. (65)

Gautama goes farther and farther from Maya, leaving Maya far behind in a state of acute psychic alienation. Gautama is not ashamed of saying before his wife: "But I am not like you. I am different from all of you." (67)

Maya's brother Arjuna who lives in New York is surprised to know that Maya is married. Maya writes to Arjuna: "I believe I am ill, something has gone wrong." She is a victim of morbid imagination:

> One of us would be left alone to always pour out his or her tea, in loneliness and I felt the shroud of death blur my vision, while through it I saw him sitting, miles away in the distance, squeezing out a small, yellow lemon that filled the stale air with a sharp, shooting odour of astringent freshness. (142)

The imagery is kinetic and throws sufficient light on the whirlwind raking in the mind of Maya. The cry of the peacock is brought to bear upon the tragic theme of this novel. Maya hears the peacock crying: "Pia, Pia," they cry. "Lover, lover. Mio, mio,—I die, I die." (95) The love of peacock is strange enough. Before they mate they fight and in course of fighting, they bleed profusely. This fact is supported by ornithology as also by religious scriptures and literary anecdotes. When the male peacock and the female peacock get themselves completely exhausted in combating, they mate. Maya thinks of their unique love: "The hundred eyes upon their tails have seen the truth of life and death." (95) The cry of the peacock symbolizes the mortal passion for love.

The peacock is wise enough. Living, they are aware of death, dying; they are in love with life. "Lover, lover." You will hear them cry in the forests when the rain-clouds come, "Lover, I die." (95-96) The cry of the peacock echoes in the ear of Maya every now and then. In a contemplative mood, she infers that there is little difference between life and death; while living the peacock is conscious of death; and while dying, they like to live. The polarity between life and death is no riddle to the peacocks. They take it as an eternal truth. The predicament of Maya is no different from that of the peacocks, while living, she suffers from death obsession and when the saw of death looms large upon her, she wants to live. Thus her position is analogous to that of the peacocks.

As tension in Maya's aberrant mind mounts, several disturbing images of creeping, crawling creatures such as rats, snakes and lizards come up one after another in close succession. These images, apart from revealing Maya's fast deteriorating psyche, illuminate some of her suffocating obsessions. The image of rats suckling their young, obliquely indicates Maya's agonizing obsession with her barrenness, childlessness:

> Rats will suckle their young most tenderly. I know this, as now I lived quite near one, with seven young ones nestling between her legs. . . . And the rats with their young, suckling them, then lashing their tails, spreading plague. (126-27)

Desai depicts Maya's psychic disorder reaching its culminating point through the image of an iguana, a large lizard with head like a snake. When Maya notices the domestic cat slinking in the room, the image of the cat gets replaced at once by that of an iguana in her mind, giving her the creeps, and she screams out scared:

> Iguanas! My blood ran cold, and I heard the slither of its dragging tail even now, in white daylight. Get off—I tell you, Get off! Go! (128)

The image of caged monkeys on the railway platform signifies Maya's loss of freedom consequent upon her marriage.

One significant stellar image which, apart from denoting the existentialist loneliness of Maya and the temperamental 'distance' between her and her elderly husband lays stress on her deep obsession with death:

> Death lurked in those spaces, the darkness spoke of distance, separation, loneliness—loneliness of such proportion that it broke the bounds of that single word and all its associations, and event spilling and spreading out and about, lapping the stars, each one isolated from the other by so much. (22)

The dance of the peacocks portrayed in chapter three; and later on referred to in chapter eleven, Part II of the novel, is indeed the most poignant of all the images used in the novel. The title of the novel also refers to this very excited dance of the peacocks at the advent of the monsoon. This image, bearing a serious significance, is remarkably relevant to the very theme of the novel. Gautama, though a father substitute for Maya, is also her lover and husband who miserably fails not only to feel the intensity of her innermost cravings but also to listen to the pathetic cry of her anguished soul, and thus when she commits suicide in the end, she, in a way, symbolically substantiates the agonized cry of the peacocks.

Papiha also finds usual mention in Indian love songs as exemplifying the idea of lovelorn beings but Papiha is not a symbol of frustration in love. The novelist refers to the cry of the peacock to denote communion ending in separation, life ending in death. While Keats' nightingale is a symbol of immortality, Desai's peacock is a symbol of life-death equation.

The hieroglyphs on her palms must come to be true sooner or later. Maya, however, believes in an incessant flowerlike life after death and in the permanence of soul. Gautama has no faith in all these. Maya is torn between two worlds—the receding one of grace, the approaching one of madness. Her body as it were breaks in the battle. Her suffering is too deep for tears. On the one hand she wants to live, on the other she wants to die. The gulf is unbridgeable. Gautama and Maya have been living for the last four years under the same roof. But it has been the impression of Maya that Gautama has throughout been blind towards her. "He was blind, blind, could not and did not care to see, to hear. Bu then, it was better so. He must not know, not even guess. Never, never, never." (151) The repetition of the word 'never' by Maya reminds us of the repetition of the same word four times by King Lear in Shakespeare's tragedy. But there is a difference. While Lear cries out of utter despair born out of his own folly at the death of Cordelia, Maya cries at the folly of Gautama which is also most irredeemable. The remarkable feature of the story of *Cry, the Peacock* is that Maya is shown how she has no grievance against her hus band at last. She is reconciled to her fate. Gautama is no more than a "figure of granite" to her. (201)

Gautama and Maya walk side by side. Maya is overwhelmed with grief when she passes through the lime tree where her pet dog lies buried. She feels that 'figure in white' is beckoning her. She turns back and looks at the frail constitution of her husband who appears to her like "a disembodied spirit clothed in off-white and frayed tie" (197). When the couple come back home, Gautama expresses his desire to take bath: "Maya—go and turn on my bath, will you?" (199) Like an obedient wife, Maya does as her husband likes. After taking bath, Gautama comes to the bed room. His anemic figure provokes Maya's peals of laughter. Gautama puts a question: "What makes you laugh?" Maya replied: "The sight of the helpless male, I presume." (199) Gautama defends: "But do not presume, no one must presume, that our marriage was an empty one, a failure." (201) Maya tacitly accepts it. But how can she forget that right from the very beginning, she has been neglected by her husband. The sense of alienation lies deep in her unconscious which always keeps her restless. She has no hesitation in admitting: "there were countless nights when I had been tortured by a humiliating sense of neglect of loneliness, of desperation that would not have existed, had I loved him so, had not meant so much." (201)

The novelist here dives deep into the psychology of woman. Love is a matter of reciprocation. It is a two-way traffic. Love must start forth as spontaneously as a bud from tree. It cannot be one-sided. The love of Maya is one-sided. It is not properly reciprocated by Gautama. He neglects her, humiliates her and thus subjects her to mental torture. The gulf between the couple is so great that it is impassable. Her agony is unspeakable. She is humiliated beyond measure but she tolerates everything with exemplary resilience. In a state of compromise with her husband, Maya says: "He is right, I am wrong." (201)

Maya feels the pangs of alienation all her life. Even when her husband is about to die, she feels the strain of aloofness. She served a cup of tea to her husband who is soon to breathe his last. Gautama is at home in the company of his wife. But Maya does not feel that she is in the company of her husband. She likes to touch her husband's forehead to comfort him. She wants to alleviate his pain by speaking a few sweet loving words. But something dissuades her from doing so.

> I longed to question him about it to touch his temples and sooth the pain, with caresses and words. But, of course, did not do so, couldn't dream of doing so. And yet the alienation, the strain of remaining aloof did not hurt. This was as it had to be. "Poor Gautama." I murmured, and with murmuring that was content. (194)

Maya stares at the pale face of her husband. "He looks like an antic owl from whose beak its prey has been snatched." (194)

The two words 'beak' and 'prey' are ambivalent. Gautama always feels that Maya was no more than a prey to her. He always kept her, not as a life partner, but as an edible material to be eaten. Again, the words 'antic owl,' are no less suggestive. Gautama is an 'antic owl,' an ugly carnivorous bird with queer behaviour, with his passing away, Maya will be released for ever, as a prey inside the beak of the bird is freed. Gautama no longer will be able to create anguish in her by his indifference and aloofness. The use of double *entendré* enhances the effect of the description. A similar double *entendré* is used by Shakespeare in his tragic play *Macbeth* when Macbeth, whose heart is full of the milk of human kindness, inches his way forward to murder king Duncan, as if a domestic crow is converted into a wild rook living on flesh.

> Come, sealing night,
> Scarf up to the tender eye of pitiful day,
> And with the bloody and invisible hand
> Cancel and tear to pieces that great bond
> Which keeps me pale.[6]

Then again the storm scene at the end of the novel *Cry, the Peacock* recalls the scene of whirlwind in Shakespeare's *King Lear*. The whirlwind described in *King Lear* projects the whirl-wind raking in the mind of King Lear.

> Blow, winds, and cracks your cheeks: rage! Blow;
> You cataracts and hurricanes, spurt till you have
> Drenched our sleepless, drownd's the cocks.[7]

In a contemplative mood Maya thinks of her miserable plight. She pretends to smile. Gautama pays no heed to her smile. Gautama is now destined to die. Maya looks at him as if she is looking at a departing guest.

> Poor man. Poor Gautama, my husband. I spoke these words in order to stop staring, to make myself feel something for him. Gautama, my husband. I rose and went up to him, beginning to feel as tenderly solicitous towards him as towards a departing guest who might never be encountered again, and I strolled with him slowly across the lawn, feeling that an unreal ghost stalked beside me—a body without a heart, a heart without a body—what was he? (196)

Besides this, Gautama was anaemic. Maya feels sorry for his posture. She knew that her husband is emotionless, sensationless. "And I felt sorry, infinitely sorry for him, for this slow, harmless, guileless being who walked the fresh grass and did not know he touched it." (197)

Similarly, the scene of storm at the end of the novel has a symbolic significance. It projects the hailstorm going on in the mind of Maya. The storm recedes, it brings cooler night. The strain on the mind of Maya is over. Maya says: "At least it's cooler now. . . . After that storm. (194)

Gautama lives with Maya but he does not know whom he is living with. This kind of narcissistic tendency coops him up within his own self. He cannot look beyond his nose. This characteristic tenet of Gautama is brought out by the novelist in the expression: "he walked the fresh grass and did not know he touched it." Maya is a 'fresh grass,' an innocent harmless girl knowing nothing of evil or wrong in this world. She is married to Gautama. But Gautama fails to appreciate her sentiments. This causes a chasm between the two.

Maya catches the sight of the Bronze Shiva—the God of destruction, "The powerful, slightly bent leg and the firm rooting of the graceful foot upon the swirling body of evil." (203) Maya sees death face to face. In a state of frustration, she pushes Gautama from the terrace. She experiences the pangs of death when her husband Gautama relinquishes his earthly body. Maya's heart is broadened. Maya knows that this world is no more than an illusion, a Maya: "Maya—my very name means nothing, is nothing, and is nothing but an illusion." (172) The dangerous prophecy of the astrologer comes true. The story ends with the tragic death of Gautama. "Maya is like an old, worn ship, breasting the waves of a terrible but well known and much traversed ocean." (64)

The cry of the peacock evokes our auditory imagination, the anecdote associated with the cry of the peacock has much to do with the life of Maya. The theme of the novel is psychic alienation. Maya, the chief female character of the novel, is psychically alienated from the very beginning of the novel. She wants to get united with her husband, but something comes in between to hinder her progress. Her alienation lingers on. The story ends with the death of Gautama.

The tragedy occurs due to a lack of communication between Maya and others. The lack of understanding and communication between individuals is echoed every now and then. In Maya's words: "There was not one of my friends who could act as an anchor anymore, and to whomsoever I turned for reassurance, betrayed me now." (64) Neither father nor husband, nor friends could remove this terrible feeling of desolation. The novel is an excellent exploration into the trauma of intense alienation. Maya is a powerful embodiment of the hauntingly cruciating loneliness. She is an archetypal stranger in the crowded world of dehumanized creatures. She is an eloquent metaphor of incommunication, unexcelled in the history of Indian English novel.

In the preceding section of this chapter, an endeavour has been made to discuss how Anita Desai, a psychic mariner, is well up in describing the feelings, emotions and sentiments of a woman who lives a life of complete alienation. In this section, the unspeakable agony of Sita, a counterpart of Maya is brought out by the novelist in all subtleties. The novelist, being a woman is better accomplished to describe the heart and mind of a woman, who is alienated not only from her husband, children and family but also from her environment. Attia Hosain, another woman novelist, in her novel *Sunlight on a broken Column* skilfully describes the transformation in her character Leila, an orphan girl. She handles the theme of a woman's agony in such a deft manner as is beyond the capacity of a male writer. In describing the emotional upsurge of a woman, Anita Desai is unparalleled.

Anita Desai's *Where Shall We Go This Summer?* is a powerful novel dealing with the predicament of a young sensitive woman named Sita who unfortunately falls a prey to self-deceit. She is fed up with the drudgery of life finding no way out of it. The whole plot of the novel hinges around Sita, the heroine of this novel, the central point of interest in the novel. From the very beginning to the end of the story, Sita remains a highly susceptible woman to whatever goes around her. As the story proceeds we notice her gradual emotional breakdown and psychic withdrawal from this world which tell upon her health and mind. She hangs between married life and her self-fulfillment while she is awaiting the birth of her fifth child. Her experiences of a housewife as well as of a mother culminate in deep anguish and agony. Her marital life is completely shaken. Her hopelessness rises and makes her insensitive, cruel and alien to her husband and children. The casual way in which her husband and children accept cruelty disturb her. Like Gautama, her husband Raman is a practical man. He is brisk and precise in dealing with business of life. Sita's emotional outbursts are beyond his comprehension. Sita does not want her fifth baby because she feels it is inhuman to bring another life into this cruel world. She goes away to Manori, the magic island where she had spent her childhood, to achieve the miracle. She is termed mad. In plain words she tells her husband: "What I am doing is trying to escape from the madness here, escape to a place where it might be possible to be sane again."[8]

The novel, *Where Shall We Go This Summer?* is the fourth novel in the series of Anita Desai's novels published in the year 1975. The novel is the shortest but it has been welcomed as "an interesting addition to Anita Desai's achievement as an Indian novelist writing in English."[9] The novelist got the federation of Indian Publishers and Author's Guild of India Award for Excellence in 1979 for writing *Where Shall We Go This Summer?*. Madhusudan Prasad considers it to be "wonderful poetic *tour de force* singularized by her intense lyrical fervour and wild poetic imagination which do not run riot but instead remain under a certain curious discipline."[10]

Structurally, the novel is quite similar to that of Virginia Woolf's *To the Lighthouse*. As in Woolf's novel, there are three parts in Desai's novel too—part one, Monsoon '67, Part two, Winter '47:, Part three, Monsoon '67 . Each section is thus concerned with a particular season, time and space. The action of the first section takes place on island Manori which is the present time of Sita's life, that of the second is her past, and the third is what she has accepted as her future. The manipulation of time and space to depict the extraordinary inner consciousness of Sita is especially reminiscent of Woolf in *To the Lighthouse*.

The novelist implies the popular flashback method in this novel. The incidents are connected more by association than by logical sequence. This is the technique, employed by James Joyce in *Ulysses* and Virginia Woolf in *To the Lighthouse* or *Mrs. Dalloway*. The incidents in the life of Sita and her visual, mental and emotional impressions are set down from moment to moment in the style of Dorothy Richardson with a touch of Joyce.

The story of the novel is spread over a period of twenty years. The novel begins where it ends, that is to say, in the very beginning of the novel we find Sita in a completely worn out and alienated position. She seems to have been torn bit by bit. Every incident which takes place in her life adds to the cracks of the already battered urn.

The story of the novel is set against the background of Manori Island in Bombay. Sita's marriage to Raman was not settled through proper understanding and love between them. Her marriage was settled: "and finally out of pity, out of lust, out of a sudden will for adventure and because it was inevitable—married her." (99) She was hardly twenty years old when she was married to Raman. Now, of course, when she revisits her village home, near Manori Island, she is forty. She has wrinkles on her face and her hair has turned grey. Raman and Sita have been living together in spite of the fact that their ideas are contradictory. This leads to disastrous consequences. There is complete lack of understanding between the couple. One could easily notice how Sita acts and reacts against the chain of circumstances in which she finds herself completely misfit. She oscillates between the two opposite poles. On the one hand there is the urge to overcome the sophistication and hypocrisy of the middle class society in which she is born and on the other there is the desire, conscious or unconscious to cling to it. She cannot so easily forsake the tie that binds her to her existence. She struggles against the oddities of life, against what may be called the uncongenial atmosphere in which she is placed. The canker of boredom slowly and gradually eats up the vitals of her soul. She loses the zest for life. She is left no more than an oil-cake. She receives jerks and jolts in her life which adversely affect her mental make up and in the end she is destitute of all mirth and gaiety of life. Every twig that composes her family nest is ruthlessly destroyed. She is caught in the whirlpool of situations beyond her control.

Sita's position is basically different from that of Isabel Archer, the heroine of Henry James' novel *The Portrait of a Lady*. Although like Sita, Isabel Archer is overshadowed by a feeling that she is destined to unhappiness, her foreboding is realised when she falls under the influence of the slightly sinister Madame Merle and is persuaded to marry the spiteful dilettante Gilbert Osmond. Osmond is only concerned with getting Isabel's fortune into his hands and he ruins her life, robbing her of any prospect of happiness and enjoyment. Although she realises his vileness, Isabel insists on remaining loyal to him. Sita too, like Isabel, remains loyal to her husband Raman despite all traumatic and appalling differences.

Where Shall We Go This Summer? is full of promise, and in its subtlety of characterization and its superb descriptive powers, it is without a rival. Anita Desai has explicitly presented the sense of loneliness in this novel. Sita's condition is representative of the loneliness of a woman, a wife, a mother, a loneliness conditioned by family and society. Sita's mental disturbances are direct result of clash between the hypocritical world and her inherent honesty that resist any such compromise. Sita's condition is symbolic of the unveiled loneliness of a modern woman in the garb of a wife, a mother and a daughter. This loneliness is conditioned by her family and society in general. Her neurosis is the direct result of clash and compromise. There remains no doubt about the fact that Sita's neurosis springs from the monotonous existence of her daily, routine married life, that denies her any sense of active involvement. Her life is a long wait for the climax that would shatter this placidity of a comfortable existence. 'Life had no periods, no stretches. It simply swirled around muddling and confusing, leading nowhere.' (155) This estrangement, the sense of separation, the loss of feeling and sympathy push her to a peculiar position where tension becomes the way of her life. As no body can live in a state of perpetual tension, unless he or she is abnormal, Sita too grows abnormal in her gesture and behaviour. The description of her unusual life forms the principle theme of this novel and it has been so deftly woven into the texture of this novel that one simply feels amazed at the narrative of the novelist, who like a subtle psychologist gives us the minutest details of Sita's uncommon existence. We watch every bit of Sita's behaviour with curiosity. At last we come to the inevitable and inexorable conclusion that for Sita there is nothing unnatural or abnormal. What she does or thinks is properly justified by the situation. Sita is almost a shamble moving on the earth. She lives and yet lives not. She is in a fix to decide what to do? She cannot put-up with her husband or children peacefully and in a harmonious manner, at the same time she cannot retrace her steps to a noble way of life.

The story of the novel begins with a vivid description of Sita's return to her village home with her children. She, being the daughter of the master of the house and since she is coming after a long gap of twenty years, is much awaited by Moses, the caretaker. However, Sita is disappointed with them and the islanders are equally disappointed with her. There are impossible expectations on both sides. She dislikes the dirt and filth of the village which lie as a sharp contrast to the comforts of her flat in Bombay. The Manori Island has of course, some attraction for her. It gives her solace, peace and satisfaction. She wants to be here all alone to mitigate her suffering, anguish and mental conflict.

Sita is in the family way, she has already given birth to four children. This is the fifth time when she is pregnant. But the boredom of her life persists. The pregnancy is at an advanced stage. Sita is so much broken from within that she at times thinks of keeping the child and sometimes thinks of not keeping it. "I mean I want to keep it—I don't want it to be born." (35)

Her pregnancy adumbrates the frothing agony. Her perplexity coupled with her disturbed conjugal life precipitates into a disastrous situation and causes aberration of her mind. Her husband, Raman, is not in a position to account for her madness, he is opposed to abortion.

> He had not read the Vedas or the Mahabharata, nothing more than scattered verses from the *Bhagwad Gita*—still, he was born a Hindu. Family planning was all very well, but not—you should have thought of it earlier, he said. It is too late now. (34)

In fact, Raman cannot gulp Sita's idea of abortion. He has instinctive hatred for his wife. He has violent dislike for her every gesture. "He hated her, hated her talk." (34)

But Sita is determined to go to her village home, the Manori village in order to escape the drudgery of life. Sita frankly admits: "What I'm doing is trying to escape from the madness *here*, escape to a place where it might be possible to be sane again." (35) When her husband tries to dissuade her from her purpose, she casts a ferocious glare at him and says: "It can happen in real life, Raman." (36) By implication, she means that life is made up of dilemma and one has to choose between two courses of action. Life is not a straight line. It has many curves and turns. She says so because she has herself undergone many odd situations in life which have strained her heart. And in order to lend support to her conviction, she recites a couplet from a poem composed by Cavafy: *"To certain people there comes a day / When they must say the Great Yes or the Great No*." (37)

Sita is put in a situation in which she can neither adjust nor rebel. She is tethered to the values which it is impossible for her to forsake. But at the same time it is difficult for her to survive in a society with these values.

When Sita was married to Raman, she was in her dreamland, now when she once again comes to her village after twenty years, she is old and exhausted, she is almost a spent-up force. She has come to the island in order not to give birth to her fifth child. We always find her in a mood of self-analysis and self-identification. She looks at the muddy sea in a perturbed state of mind:

> She began restlessly turning, looking into the muddy sea as if to pierce its depth and discover its treasure, then at the island, then at the sky as still and rigid as a boil slowly gathering to bursting point. (18)

It is evident from the behaviour of the children that they are unlike their mother. Contrary to the restlessness of Sita who often bursts into violent eruptions of emotions, her children are mild, quiet-looking almost like stone statues. They have still to see this world: "Unlike their mother, who continually broke apart into violent eruptions of emotion, the children seemed rigid, encased in their separate silences like larvae in stiff-spun cocoons." (19) The simile is highly suggestive. Cocoon means the silken covering made by the caterpillars or usually by the silk worms in order to protect themselves from outer attacks. The position of the children is no better than those tiny insects. They keep quiet because this is the only medium by which they can protect themselves. They observe silence because this is the only way to provide shelter for them but this silence is actually indicative of their inward turmoil. Disturbance is brewing within them and it is not known when and how it would come up in all its fury and ugliness. When there is conjugal rift between husband and wife, the growth of the children is automatically stilted. There is a clear indication that the children lack mutual trust and co-ordination and discipline.

> Their language he could not follow at all but he had expected the tone of their conversation to give him a lead and inform him why they had come. It gave him none—except that there were rifts and dissensions in the family as he had known there would be, must be, since there was no father to hold them together and lead them in obedience, nor even a husband. (20)

Sita no doubt has her husband, the children are not fatherless but the discord in the family separated each member of the family from the other. Sita hardly feels that she has her husband. The children scarcely realize that they have a father to control them. Sita is in the habit of disagreeing with her husband on every vital issue of life. She abhors her village because life there is not picturesque. She is full of praise for her flat at Queens Roads in Bombay containing all modern amenities:

> White with electric light, the twinkle of China, the meal served by servants in white, the routine to which the children were used, and their beds, smooth, cool. (29)

Life in the village becomes intolerable to her. She hysterically cries 'help me.' She is in love with the sophistication and decency of the middle-class society. She takes to smoking only to cover up her guilt, to put a cloak on her frailties and to some extent to get peace and mitigate her tension. She smokes twice when she feels the atmosphere of the village ill suits her mind, trained in cultural thinking;

> Guilt wore her out. She finally sat down at the table and fed them biscuits and the milk Moses brought in a brass vessel, watched them nibble and sip in silence while she smoked a string of cigarettes. Stamping them under foot, she got them up, changed them, put them to bed with her last reserve of strength, moving already semi-

> consciously, like a zombie. She sat for a while at the edge of Karan's bed, smoking another cigarette, as though this last one may convey an assurance or an answer, then lay down at his side in a heap. (30)

The story of Sita's father is an integral part of the fabric of the novel. Sita's father is looked upon as a fable on the Manori Island. He is a name for his skill in herbs and medicine. Apart from this, there is a hear-say that he is quite at home in witchcraft and necromancy. It is said that he has cured millions of people who were otherwise incurable. Barren ladies were blessed with sons by the mercy of this old wizard. A motherless child, she experiences neglect and uncertainties right through her childhood. "His *chelas* called him a saint, his critics a charlatan, the villagers a wizard, and each produced evidence to prove his theory." (75)

In this way, there is mixed reaction to the dealings of Sita's father. While he is admired and held in high esteem by some persons, he is considered a hoax, a man simply pretending to possess greater skill than others in handling abnormal cases. Sita is indifferent to the activities of her father particularly because her father is indifferent to the activities of his offsprings. Love is reciprocal. It is an object of give and take. Unfortunately, love is denied to Sita from both sides, from the side of her father as well as from her mother. She feels lonely and isolated in this wide world.

Sita's situation is just the reverse of Maya's in *Cry, the Peacock*. If Maya's father is over-protective that creates a conflicting situation, Sita's father neglects her completely. He has no time for his children. A public figure, admired and revered by the people, he is too far off and formidable a person for Sita to approach with filial affection. The atmosphere, in which Sita lives and grows, is that of neglect, hypocrisy and partiality, consciously as well as unconsciously, she is uneasy. She does not have the feeling of belongingness. Involvement can be with another person, an idea or a group. Erich Fromm maintains that by uniting himself with other person in the spirit of life and shared work, man can hope to end his alienation. A family is the most important internal group to condition a person's relationship to himself. R.D. Zaing considers family to be internalized in one of us. It is like a flower, with mother as the centre, the children as its petal around it. The vital link—the mother—is missing in Sita's life. This leads to an alienation from self. Her vague fears, an abiding sense of dissatisfaction, nausea and mortal dread to taking on responsibility of the newcomer—all point towards the sense of insecurity bred in childhood. She comes to Manori Island not for fun or recreation but for begging for 'miracle' of keeping her baby 'unborn.' (31)

Sita knows that she is becoming uncontrolled and unbridled in her behaviour. She adopts a defiant attitude towards all. There are persons who take to drinking in order to relieve themselves of their worries. Sita takes to smoking in order to forget her surroundings.

Right from the beginning of her married life, Sita has been feeling the pricks of the inharmonious behaviour of her husband. Slowly and gradually, she becomes an introvert.

> She never got used to anyone. Then they lived, in their first years of their married life, with his family in their age-rotted flat of Queens Road, she had vibrated and throbbed in revolt against their subhuman placidity, calmness and sluggishness. . . . She behaved provocatively—it was there that she started smoking. (48)

> She took to smoking instead of eating, to staring about her silence, to speaking provocatively. (49)

> She spent almost all her time on their balcony, smoking, looking out at the sea. (50)

Raman is an ordinary simple human being whereas Sita like Maya is an over-sensitive woman. Both are ill matched. Raman fails to understand her:

> Control was an accomplishment that had slipped out of her hold, without his noticing it, over the years, till now she had no more than an infant has before he has begun the process of acquiring it, and so she wept and flung herself about. (32)

The partial life of Sita is an awful tale of inhibitions and separations. She never indulges in open confrontation with Raman.

> All through their married life, they had preferred to avoid confrontation. All that they had done, he now saw, was to pile on the fury till now when it exploded. (33)

But this leads to an entirely different result. The fury piles "up till now when it exploded." When Sita dauntlessly says that she does not like her fifth child to be born, it simply puzzled her husband. When Sita asserts, "But I don't *want* to have the baby," (34) it simply sends a tremor into the soul of her husband. Raman distinctly remembers how

> She stood all day on the balcony keeping away the crows that were attacking a wounded eagle on a neighbouring roof top, and who winced dreadfully every time she heard a child cry. (34)

Not to have a baby is repugnant to the nature and character of a woman and therefore, Raman is taken aback when Sita pronounces she has no liking for a new baby. The statement of Sita seems to bear nothing but brutality and murderousness. The image of the crows attacking a wounded eagle is strikingly original. The wounded heart of Sita is being attacked again and again. Her heart bleeds. Crows from all round seem to make her wound fresh and more aching by their beaks. The image is Shakespearean in dimension. In *Macbeth* we have the image of the crows making way to rooky woods. The image is implied in the context of Macbeth whose personality undergoes a complete metamorphosis. From a man whose heart is full of the milk of human kindness, he turns a blood-thirsty man with no pity and human sympathy.

The domestic and gregarious crow becomes a rook living on flesh. In the present description by the novelist, the image of the crows has been implied with a certain difference. The crows attacking a wounded eagle suggest the constant onslaught on the tender feelings of Sita who is already in an injured state. Raman is not in favour of abortion; he tells Sita that now it is too late to think of abortion, she should have thought of it earlier. It is clearly hinted at in the novel that Raman hates his wife on this score but there is no escaping this situation. Raman cannot persuade himself to make a compromise with his wife on this point when he insists that she ought to take care of the baby in her womb, she loses the poise and balance of her mind. The whole episode is charged with imagination. The hot exchange of words between the husband and wife is dramatic:

> They stared, uncomprehendingly, at each other, more divided than they had been on the balcony that day—she fighting, the other laughing. What did he mean? What did she mean? In that snarled moment of silence, time was scummy sea, telling nothing. (34)

Sita's grief is too deep for tears. She is well nigh mad. The mental derangement of Sita is skilfully brought out by the novelist in her seemingly contradictory statement: "I want to keep it, I don't want it to be born." (35)

She rebels against the 'vegetable existence' lived by the women in Raman's family: "As far as Sita could tell from her own experience, their lives had been lived inside jails, in crowded assemblies, in mobs, in slums, tenements, and villages where life was not picturesque or calm, but harsh and barbaric. . . . There had been long separations, dark seclusions. There had been austerity and fear. It was always made clear to Sita that this was no age for games or sweets but one for prayer and sacrifice. Having no true alternative, she accepted it." (35)

In one's life, there is a time for orgy and merry-making when everything looks colourful. Then a time comes when one ceases interest in outward phenomena and turns inward. It is the time for self-contemplation, meditation and renunciation. Sita is physically young. But circumstance has made her mentally and psychologically old. Her weird and unnatural thinking is the outcome of her broken life. Even while she is young, she thinks of prayer and sacrifice. Once Phoolmaya, a worshipper of Sita's father, calls on Sita and brings something for her. She is shocked to see her shrivelled face. She does not like to remind Sita of her wrinkled skin: "She did not wish to refer to that age or that scene; it would be ludicrous and cruel to try link them to the woman who stood there." (76) Initially, it is only verbal attack, then she takes recourse to a more flagrant disregard for their way of life, by taking to smoking shocking them thus, Sita enjoys a sense of superiority. She feels like a square peg in a round hole. Unable to adjust herself with them, she moves to a flat and lives alone with her husband and children. Her life is hardly better, her privacy is disturbed. She finds her existence at stake; she struggles with the monotony of life. Raman is startled when she describes his business associates as animals: "They are nothing—nothing but appetite and sex, only food, sex and money matter. Animals." (105) Sita does not relish the drab and commonplace talk of the professional businessman. To her, these business men have 'sub human' character. Even her husband is hardly above that category. One immediately recalls Maya in *Cry, the Peacock*. Like Sita, Maya shows her disgust for the people and the entire atmosphere at the Lal's party. Gautama is irritated and he exhorts her to learn to bear everyday mediocrity. Sita also baffles Raman by her behaviour and she enjoys having thus annoyed him. It gives her a sense of triumph. Raman wants to suppress the feeling of his wife by bullying her and by subjecting her to the most dishonourable position. The result is that she speaks in sudden rush of emotions. She spends most of her time on the balcony, smoking, looking at the sea. She is completely cut off from the rest of the family. She has everything and she has nothing. She even forgets that she was once married; she looks at her wedding photograph, she can hardly recognize herself as a bride. The disharmony in her marital life takes her too far from her husband and children. This sense of acute alienation and isolation on the part of Sita is excellently described by the novelist in a series of images:

> She seemed to have adopted, for the occasion—the way an insect might adopt certain characteristics not of its own breed for the sake of camouflage and self-defence—the anonymous look of a shy, not wholly conscious bride quite unlike her appearance at any other time. It was a look, she had immediately discarded and lost. She was amused to turn from the album to the mirror and see the layers of experience and melancholy and boredom that had settled upon her face since then, like so much grey sand. (47)

Sita is destroyed from within and without. Every fibre of her life is spoilt beyond repair. Destruction comes to her so naturally that she is hardly aware of the fact that she is being destroyed: "destruction that had begun with time and was now roaring around her, battering her and her fish-foetus so that survival seemed hopeless." (55)

Sita's mind moves on a rational plane. She thinks that she is right in her own way. She thinks that by giving birth to a baby, she will not be performing an act of creation. On the contrary, she would only be indulging in an act of destruction because thereby she would destroy the newly born child in a violent world, who is all safe in the womb. The demarcating line between construction and destruction seems to dwindle before her: "The line between the creative and the destructive grew so thin, so hazy and undefinable that, gazing at it, she seemed to see it vanish altogether." (55)

Sita has all along been subjective in her preoccupations. She has her own way to tackle a problem. She does not care if her views are not supported by others. In fact, she needs no support, for good or for bad—she has her own standard of judgment, scale of assessment. Her precarious position can be well realized from her attitude to life and death. She loves her mother very much. Her mother is dead but she feels her life is incomplete without her, she is not attached to anyone whether he is her father, her husband or anybody else. Nothing is precious to her: "Life seemed complete, full, without her; there was no reason for her to exist." (56)

Sita's fabled father is no more but she remains completely unaffected. She does not feel the loss. She does not like even the biography of her father to be written to commemorate his memory. The life of Sita's father has been eventful throughout. At last his biography is written by his friends and admirers. However, in this biography, Rekha, Sita's eldest sister, is praised in high-flown words for her singing skill for which she is deservedly called the Nightingale of the All India Radio and something is written on Jivan, Sita's younger brother. Only a single line is written on Sita who miserably fails to distinguish in any walk of life:

> The facts were dull, repetitive and, in spite of the many references to people she had known, did not interest her. Magnetic in life, after his death he seemed turned into a cold lump of metal by his biographers. (84)

As the story proceeds, Sita is gradually removed from the usual surroundings and associations, she is turned from an affectionate attitude to an indifferent, unfriendly or even a hostile one. She deliberately opts for illusion in place of reality. She cannot face the stern realities of life. She returns again and again to Manori Island for peace and solace. She cannot go elsewhere, when this time the question crops up before her—where shall we go this summer?

Sita unhesitatingly says that she would go to Manori Island, her favourite place:

> Knowing that, accepting that, she knew it was because ordinary life, the every day world had grown so insufferable to her that she could think of the magic island again as of release. If the sea is so dark, so cruel then it was better to swim back into the net. If reality were not to be borne, then illusion was the only alternative. She saw that island, illusion as a refuge, a protection. It would hold her baby safely unborn, by magic. (89)

In fact, Sita is in a state of indecision. The interrogation, where shall we go this summer?, indicates that Sita is not able to decide where to go. One might assume that she had finally made up her mind to go to her Manori village in order to have rest and peace there "as for a rest in a sanatorium." (89) The peace is intrinsic rather than extrinsic. No place can afford peace to a man whose mind is restless. Sita's mind knows no rest. It is always disturbed on account of her disrupted conjugal life. Place does not matter. If the mind is lacking in poise and equilibrium even heaven cannot give peace and happiness to a man. "Where shall we go this summer? the words appearing out of nowhere, worried her and plagued her. 'Nowhere, nowhere' she made an effort to control herself and quietly reply: 'I'll keep you safe inside. Will go nowhere,' soothing herself, reassuring herself, she silenced the doubts and walked more slowly till there entered into her mind again those wavering, disconnected lines she still could not place or recapture." (101)

This conflict is the product of duality in her mind. She is not certain what to do. Her mind rambles from one point to another taking her nowhere: "She felt surrounded by presence—the presence of the island itself, of the sea around it, and of the palm trees that spoke to each other and, sometimes, even to her." (126) The island house, deserted for twenty years, symbolizes her temperamental conditions. As Vimala Rao aptly suggests, "The island concretizes the feeling of isolation of Sita. She retreats into it as into a womb, with an obsessive desire to recapture once again her childhood innocence and purity . . . obviously, her own frustration with her life in Bombay drives her in her desire to provide her unborn infant with a world that is uncorrupt." (50) Sita's agony is deep; her life is cut as under by an invisible force. Sita is not in a position to put up comfortably even with her children: "She had herself almost ceased to believe in magic, in life, in animation" (108)

Sita is like a barren tree. Alienation and separation dry up the leaves before time. Now, she has lost her faith not only in liveliness but in life. Gloom surrounds her from all the corners. Sita develops death obsession:

> For some years then death occupied her and terrified her as it should not any but the doomed, and Sita had been too incompetent a mother to know how to deal with her trauma, how to give her comfort; there was none, and it was not in her to concoct any. (108)

The episode of Sita's fear of death invites a comparison with a similar episode described by William Faulkner in his novel *As I Lay Dying*. The narrative is spun out of the web of much delayed burial of a woman by members of her family. One of the characters in the novel is a girl with curious ideas of death and what has become of her coffin mother. Anita Desai, however, describes the death obsession of Sita with a difference while the young girl described by William Faulkner in *As I Lay Dying* is unable to understand what death is and what happens after death, Sita knows that death means complete annihilation of earthy existence. The shadow of death hangs heavy upon her. This is because she is annoyed with her living, with her environment and with her existence.

Once Sita's daughter Menaka expresses her desire to her mother that she would like to become a scientist. Sita sharply reacts:

> "Oh science, Menaka! Sita's knee jerked nervously. "Science can't be as satisfactory. It's all figures, statistics, logic. Science is believing that two and two make four—pooh," she exhaled a mouthful of acrid smoke in blatant disgust.
>
> "Nothing, nothing, it's a mask, a shroud, nothing else." (116)

When Sita has denied her own self, it is but natural that she should be abnormal in her behaviour. The story of Sita is the story of a woman who is a living corpse. Sita dreads her own shadow. She does not believe in anything whether it is science, politics or any other deliberation. She even does not believe in her own self. Her mental conflict, her tortured ego, her sombre thinking, and above all, the jerks and jolts in her life are picture sequel described by the novelist in their minutest details as a painter does with his brush.

Sita at last breaths a sigh of relief that after all she lost everything. She is like "a white bird, flying up with one strident scream, then plummeting down thinking it's all over." (108) As in Desai's earlier novels *Cry, the Peacock* and *Voices in the City* in which Maya and Monisha respectively crack up eventually under the pressure of urban domesticity, Sita too reaches a near breakdown.

But at last, much to her chagrin, Sita understands that she cannot say great 'No' mentioned in the poem of Cavafy that has for ever been carved on her mind. She is a failure, she is crushed. Raman who has come to the island is unconvinced by her arguments and reasons of coming to the island. As he prepares to leave for the main land, Sita feels insecure and unprotected once again. In portraying Sita, who is opposed to society and forces of life, and by stressing her inner conflicts, Anita Desai gives the impression that life in spite of the contraries that assail it, has to be lived because 'the existent life is in constant interaction with other existences or existence is being with others.' Life full of treasons, betrayals and treacheries cannot be avoided. These are elements that penetrate a person as air and water do. It struck Sita then, that Raman too has suffered from worry and anxiety about her, the unborn child. It was her consummate glimpse into the human psyche. While walking on the beach, she began to trail after him: "Knowing she would follow him, follow the trail of foot prints he had laid out for her." (150) She realized:

> Her time on the island had been very much of an episode on a stage, illuminated by gaudy sunset effects and played to thunderous storm music. The storm ended, the play over, the stage had now to be cleared. (152)

Instead of living a life of primitive reality on a false stage, she was now to return to a life of retirement, off-stage." (153) She had realized the difference between the necessity and the wish, between what a man wants and what he is compelled to do. Her desire to bear the child and return with Raman to the main land signifies her return to life, community and society in spite of the debased dullness of life, the calamity, the lies and moral buggery, and sorrow dropped on every heart, for existence is not possible in an insulated stage of being, rather existence implies being with other.

Ironically, Sita herself looks at her life on the island as an episode on the stage. But then, her married life too appears to her as a life of pretence and performance. The line of demarcation between reality and illusion is so thin that one overlaps the other. Having understood the wisdom of Raman's practicality, she decides to accept life as it is. Sita who has come to the island as a dark and threatening monsoon cloud, wild and passionate, now achieves calmness and quietude. Sita is an improvement over Maya (*Cry, the Peacock*) and Monisha (*Voices in the City*) in that she ultimately finds a compromise, a meeting point between Maya's involvements, in her realization that there is no freedom and fulfillment without enchantment. Speaking of the ending of the novel, Suresh Kohli rightly points out that as compared to her earlier works there is "one distinct change. Sita neither dies in the end nor kills anyone, nor does she become mad. She simply compromises with her destiny."[11] Sita learns to face life with all its ups and downs. It is after all Raman, whom she despised earlier for his practicality and matter-of-factness that taught her that

> life must be continued, and all its business—Menaka's admission to medical college gained, wife led to hospital, new child safely brought forth, the children reared, the factory seen to, a salary earned, a salary spent. (138-39)

Sita's decision to return to her husband in no sense signifies her failure. It, on the contrary, suggests that she has learnt patience and courage to face life with all its ups and down. The positive ending of the novel registers a distinct change in the novelist's outlook. It belies the commonly held opinion that Anita Desai is a novelist predominantly interested in depicting the feminine abnormal sensibility and that her heroines bring violent end to their lives.

Sita's struggle symbolizes the intelligent and sensitive woman's revolt against the male smugness and philistinism. Her final return to normal humdrum existence is suggestive of her sanity and courage and the teasing ambiguity of life.

In contrast to other novelists like Raja Rao, Mulk Raj Anand, R.K. Narayan and Bhabani Bhattacharya, Anita Desai uses a different set of language to describe the inner tensions and crises in the minds of her character. Almost all her characters are existential, non-political or social. She presents each individual as an unsolved mystery. By using first person narrative, she allows her character to tell his or her story, but nowhere the reader feels that she is manipulating her characters. Thus she chooses the method of narrating the story to meet the challenging possibilities. A trivial situation or an unimportant incident in Desai's novels evokes subjective and neurotic response, she very carefully and intelligently mixes the first person narrative with third person which sometimes helps to creative purposive contrast. She does not appear anxious to underline her own theme.

Anita Desai and Virginia Woolf have rather few themes—incompatibility of marriages and inharmonious man-woman relationships. Her psychological characters are as good as those of Miller, Richardson and James Joyce.

In Desai's characters there is a violent clash between the desire to withdraw and achieve harmony. In all her novels, there is a longing, a desire, a striving on the part of the protagonist towards finding out or arriving at a more authentic way of life than the life they lead. There is a need to be loved. Maya or Sita desire this above everything else. Though they also resist, surrender and involve, the problem of involvement or detachment or freedom has got psychological perspective. Maya's unhappiness in *Cry, the Peacock* when analysed is not the reality of her circumstances. It is a product of her own consciousness. When she is confronted with the realities of life, she gets disappointment and she is incapable of doing away with it. In each and every situation, Maya desires for a child-like consolation. She wants to be assured that all will be well with her. Maya feels lonely and neglected. She finds that nobody understands her. She acknowledges that Gautama is an ally and it is due to him that she has to suffer. There are a number of evidences in her life which force her to become a neurotic. The tension within her gives rise to severe headaches which are symptomatic of her desire to escape the issues. But reality can no longer be denied. Therefore, her own fears and thoughts crowd her mind. Her disturbed feelings puncture her patience and gradually her psyche cracks insidiously. When she looks around for some guidance, the advice available to her clashes with her inclinations.

In *Where Shall We Go This Summer?* Sita refuses to continue the life as it comes to her. It is simply the manifestation of her Bolshevik disposition. Her trip to Manori is really a retreat to her childhood. This trip for her is a trap of self-identity and recognition of reality. In her island home, she is an outsider as she was on the mainland. Her daily disappointments are numberless. Her memories of past and uncertainty of the future have created a sense of dismay and disgust in her heart. The island life is a symbol of a private refuse to her and she is in her route of escape. It was a lull before storm. The eruption was volcanic.

Where Shall We Go This Summer? is a grim book in which the alienation of a young married woman has been delineated in vivid terms. Sita is a victim of morbidity, a product of her perpetual anguish, which has a menacing effect on her mind and heart. All through she remains a riddle for her husband and also for her children. Her portrait precisely is the portrait of almost every modern woman afflicted by matrimonial maladjustment, resulting in domestic violence, separation and alienation. The relation between Sita and Raman is embittered day by day which ultimately leads to an emotional shipwreck.

Emotion, instinct, feeling, reasons occupy the central theme of all the novels of Anita Desai. The mystery remains unsolved. Her Maya and Sita confess their longing in life. They are orphans either factually or emotionally. They either disown or are disowned by their families. They come from incomplete families. Maya gets memory of her mother through her photographs on father's desk. Sita's mother has run away from her home leaving the children to the care of their father.

The story of Sita's mother is no less pathetic. Probably, she is drowned in the Ganges in Benaras. Raman, it is not known what made her abandon her husband, tries his best to locate her in Benaras. But in vain, "All efforts, all enquiries drew a blank. . . . She shrugged when her husband returned from Benaras and gave up the pursuit." (87) Sita's mother does not leave even her photograph behind her. "Sita had imagined she came into the world motherless." (84) As to Sita's father, who is nicknamed second Gandhi, a biography is written by an old lady, a copy of which is presented to Sita. Sita is shocked to learn from his biography that not 'a single line' is devoted to Sita.

While exhibiting an extraordinary skill in probing into the psyche of woman and analyzing the inner struggle in the context of husband-wife relationship, Anita Desai exercises an admirable control in that, she never shows a trace of biased or prejudiced outlook. Her women are hypersensitive and, at times, even high-strung too and they suffer because of their inability to cope with the realities of life. If Maya's introversion and introspection are necessary for the development of her character, Sita's emotional jerks account for her alienation. Nayantara Sahgal's women struggle to change the existing world order and usher in a new order, where there is no place for hypocrisy, pretence and dual morality. The women come out of the bond, if need be, to live as free individuals whereas Anita Desai's women either succumb or survive the existential problems within the family fold.

In the final analysis, Sita, the heroine of the novel *Where Shall We Go This Summer?*, emerges as the representative of all broken women of the present-day milieu whose fate can only be redeemed by social consciousness and moral awakening. Maya of *Cry, the Peacock* commits suicide, Sita of *Where Shall We Go This Summer?* succumbs to her situation in spite of herself. This is the miserable plight of the present-day woman. Anita Desai, a true existentialist, exhibits deep concern for this existence of a woman in this uncongenial social surrounding which poses a question whether to live or die. The woman struggles hard. But unless the whole social set up is changed, she can do nothing but languish bearing all excruciating agonies, mental and psychological atrocities and traumatic sufferings.

NOTES

1. Meena Belliappa, *Anita Desai, A Study of Her Fiction (*Writers Workshop, Calcutta, 1971), p. 9.
2. Anita Desai, *Cry, the Peacock* (Orient Paperbacks, 1983), p. 200.
3. K.R. Srinivasa Iyengar, *Indian Writing in English* (Sterling, New Delhi, 1984), p. 466.
4. D.H. Lawrence, 'Odour of Chrysanthemums,' *The Tales of D.H. Lawrence* (Secker, London, 1934), p. 200.
5. T.S. Eliot, *The Fire Sermon, The Waste land (*Faber & Faber, London, 1980), p. 60.
6. William Shakespeare, *Macbeth*, Act III, Scene II, lines, 46-50.
7. William Shakespeare, *King Lear*, Act III, Scene II, lines 1-3.
8. Anita Desai, *Where Shall We Go This Summer?* (Orient Paper back, Delhi, 1982), p. 35.
9. Vimala Rao, "Anita Desai's *Where Shall We Go This Summer?* An Analysis," *Commonwealth Quarterly*, December 1978, p. 50.
10. Madhusudan Prasad, *Anita Desai: The Novelist* (New Horizon, Allahabad, 1981), p. 107.
11. Suresh Kohli, "The Fiction of Anita Desai," *The Statesman*, Sunday Magazine Section, 6 Nov. 1977, p. 3.

The Ideogram of Existence
Arun Joshi's *The Foreigner*

> Look at me. I have no roots. I have no system of morality. What does it mean to me if you call me an immoral man? I have no reason to be one thing rather than another. You ask me why I am not ambitious; well, I have no reason to be. Come to think of it I don't even have a reason to live![1]

Arun Joshi's novels explicate still another dimension of alienation. His characters are archetypal outsiders. They present the predicament of the representative modern urban Indian lost in the labyrinth of life, reality and existence. Human loneliness is related to his existential crisis. Joshi's novels *The Foreigner* and *The Last Labyrinth* spell out the lower depths of human suffering and the infernal existential agony. The most exciting feature about Arun Joshi is the truth that he attempts a serious probe into the existential problems of mankind by fixing the lens of his focus on certain individualistic characters. Arun Joshi's fiction complies with Conrad's conception of the novel. Joseph Conrad recognizes a reality beyond the phenomenal world, a reality which the artist could imagine and capture by giving a consistent form to the shapeless facts of actual human existence. Joshi recognizes a reality beyond the mere phenomenal world, a reality which the artist could imagine and capture by giving a consistent form to the shapeless facts of human existence. The source of most of Joshi's novels is actual experience.

A certain awareness of man's rootlessness and the consequent loneliness and anxiety is the keynote of Arun Joshi's unique vision of the predicament of modern man. His awareness is also focused on the evils of man's material concerns. But he is against the outworn mode and style of detachment and renunciation, so laboriously built up by the Raja Rao metaphysics and its followers, Santha Rama Rau in *Remember the House*, Anita Desai in *Cry, the Peacock*, Nayantara Sahgal in *A Time to be Happy* and Sudhin Ghose in *The Flame of the Forest*. He is more emphatically concerned with the search for the essence of human living and the need for the acculturation of man to establish him back to his roots, self and peace.

Arun Joshi's first novel, *The Foreigner* explores in depth, the problems of Sindi Oberoi. O.P. Bhatnagar remarks: "A strange feeling of aloneness and aloofness . . . permeates the entire narrative and provides the necessary texture and structure to the novel.[2] In her review of the novel, Meenakshi Mukherjee describes Sindi Oberoi as 'a perennial outsider.'[3] Sindi is born of an Indian father and British mother in Kenya, who suffers philosophical, spiritual and psychological alienation. He is a rootless drifter, a foreigner wherever he goes. Sindi is brought up by his uncle because both his parents die in a plane crash near Cairo prematurely. He goes as an engineering student to Boston. Here he meets June, a loving and lovable young American woman. She falls in love with this sad-looking Indian. He also loves her, but when she talks of marriage, he shrinks back on the grounds that marriage means possession and hence attachment. He tells June:

> All love—whether of things, or persons, or oneself—was illusion and all pain sprang from this illusion. Love begot greed and attachment, and it led to possession. (171)

Sindi is a perfect foreigner. He is not only foreigner to the two cultures between which he shuttled but also to his soul. He is an orphan both in terms of relations and his emotional roots. He feels he does not belong anywhere but his rootlessness is neither geographic nor cultural. This is a personal problem of emotions seeking fulfillment in terms of human relations and existence in general. His entire view of life and responses are because of the deprivation of parental love in his childhood. Sindi, therefore, entertained a deep sense of insecurity, unreality and impermanence of life. In one of his conversations with his beloved, he says:

> I have loved people as much as I love myself. It isn't much but that is not my fault. And then to be in love in your sense requires one to take things seriously, assume that there is permanence about things.

> Nothing ever seems real to me, leave alone permanent. Nothing seems to be very important. (107)

Sindi becomes a wandering alien, rootless like Naipaul's 'unanchored souls' or Camus' 'outsider.' He is in fact, an anomie man, a consequence of social dysfunction. The theory of French socio-linguist Durkheim and the American thinker Merton on anomie is clearly spelt out by Robert M. Mac Iver: "Anomie signifies the state of mind of one who has been pulled up from his moral roots . . . who has no longer any sense of continuity of folk, of obligation. The anomie man has become spiritually sterile, responsive only to himself, responsible to no one."[4]

Oberoi's case typically represents this state of anomie or alienation, his moral vacuity, spiritual bankruptcy and apathy; he is isolated from the whole apparatus of society. He calls himself 'An uprooted young man living in the later half of the twentieth century who had become detached from everything except myself.' (195) His predicament is spelt in clear terms in his dialogue with Mr. Khemka:

> You had a clear-cut system of morality, a caste system that laid down all you had to do. You had a God; you had roots in the soil you live upon. Look at me. I have no roots. I have no system of morality . . . I have no reason to be one thing rather than another. . . . I don't even have a reason to live. (138-39)

Sindi is an alien everywhere, just like Srinivas in Kamala Markandaya's *The Nowhere Man* and Meursault in Camus' *The Outsider*. Like Meursault, Sindi is devoid of life and affection: 'Even if I loved her and she love me, it would mean nothing, nothing that one could depend upon. I was not the kind of man one could love.'

Sindi is restless everywhere—in Kenya, London and America. In Kenya, he even attempted a suicide, when he was only a boy. While studying in London he meets Anna, a minor artist separated from her husband. He has an affair with this Solo artist who yearns neither for him nor anybody, but for her lost youth. Later he is deeply involved with Mathy, an English housewife who hungers for adulterous love. She leaves Sindi after carrying on with him for a few weeks and goes back to her husband because, "She thought marriage was sacred and had to be maintained at all costs."

(169)The subsequent separation makes him realize that love was illusion and all pain sprang from this illusion. In his eagerness to find the meaning of life, Sindi lives 'in a strange world of intense pleasure and almost equally intense pain.' But he fails to make a satisfactory progress and, as he himself tells us, his twenty-five years are "largely wasted in search of wrong things in wrong places." (91)

Sindi is trapped in his own loneliness which is accentuated by his withdrawal from the society around him. He wonders:

> In what way, if any, did I belong to the world that roared beneath my window? Somebody had begotten me without a purpose and so far I had lived without a purpose, unless you could call the search for peace a purpose. Perhaps I felt like that because I was a foreigner in America. But then, what difference would it have made if I had lived in Kenya or India . . . or any other place for that matter? It seemed to me that I would still be a foreigner. My foreignness lay within me and I couldn't leave myself behind wherever I went. (61)

Sindi's sufferings are manifestations of a spiritual crisis. He wants peace, a capacity to love and the courage to live, 'without desire and attachment.' This philosophy of detachment comes to reality in his relationship with June and Babu in Boston. He gains a new life when he meets June, the American girl, beautiful and benign, with a Christ in her heart craving to be of help to someone. Their relationship gradually intensifies and Sindi's defences of detachment fall apart one after another. June's desires are homely and human. She wants to love, marry, create a home and make it a heaven as a mother to the children. June is an American girl with belief in sensate pleasure but she is also strongly fascinated by oriental transcendentalism and Indian mysticism. In her sense of sacrifice and love for the mystical, June is an embryonic Bilasia of *The Strange Case of Mr. Billy Biswas* and Anuradha of *The Last Labyrinth.*

Sindi's loneliness is apparent to everyone who meets and talks to him. His companion in the flat, Karl, once tells him: 'I didn't know you could laugh.' Sindi's reply is as significant as the remark that provoked it, 'I can if I'm drunk enough.' Sheila once says to Sindi, "You are the saddest man I have ever known." (143)

Sindi himself confesses: "I was cynical and exhausted, grown old before my time, weary with my own loneliness." (154) Babu's father Khemka is not wrong when he tells Sindi: "you are living, but as bad as dead." In their very first meeting, June tells him:

> There is something strange about you, you know. Something distant. I'd guess that when people are with you they don't feel like they are with a human being. Maybe it's an Indian characteristic, but I have a feeling you'd be a foreigner everywhere. (30)

When Sindi refuses to marry June, she has no option but to turn to Babu, who loves her intensely and needs her badly. Babu Rao Khemka has come to America for higher studies. He sees America as a paradise for fooling around with girls. He wants to make American friends rather than mixing with Indians all the time. He expresses his feeling of being born in America and says: "I would never go back to India if I had the choice." (89) If Sindi is a drifter, Babu was too much anchored to his parents. They possessed him so much that they deprived him of his free will, hampering his capacity to make resolutions and take action in tune with his growth. In America Babu becomes a split personality. He comes of an orthodox Hindu family and is unable to divest himself of its traditional ethical values to make his adjustment with American life possible. What makes Babu's situation in America still worse for him is his mortal fear of his fastidious, orthodox, and domineering father. As he has a deep respect for his father and feels obliged to him for what he has done to him, and even pretends he is not afraid of him, he has not the heart to annoy him. In this divided state of mind, he is neither able to devote himself to his studies nor able to enjoy his life in America. It is because of his moral inhibitions and orthodox background that Babu fails miserably in his relations with June and consequently drives her to her ruin and himself to his tragic death. He wishes to take June on his own terms, looking for virginal purity of an ideal Indian girl in her. He does not understand that "codes of morality differ from country to country." (55) When Babu comes to know that June, her fiancée, has been sleeping with Sindi, he is driven mad and commits suicide. After Babu's death, June discovers that she is pregnant. She undergoes an abortion and dies in the process.

Distraught and guilty, Sindi opts to go to India. A flip of the coin decides that he migrate to India, the land from where his forefathers had come. From Sindi's own reflections on his relations with June, it transpires that he loves her immensely. She stands by him in his physical troubles. She seems to be the only person who can give him emotional stability and security. Sindi cannot resist the charms of her physical attraction despite his self-imposed discipline and celibacy. However, when she proposes marriage in order to regularize and legalize their relations, he shuns the idea. He discards it by preaching the virtue of detachment. He explains to a bewildered June that marriage means possession and that he is "afraid of possessing anybody and . . . being possessed and marriage meant both." (105-6)

> Marriage wouldn't help, June. We are alone, both you and I. That is the problem. And our aloneness must be resolved from within, you can't send two persons through a ceremony and expect that their aloneness will disappear. (124)

This attitude of Sindi estranges June from him. Babu had given her all she needed. She could be of use to him and he loved her with dog-like devotion. Above all, he needed her. This was a trump that June could not resist Babu. She dangles between Babu and Oberoi. She cannot put up with Sindi's philosophy of detachment and transitoriness of love. She discusses it with Sindi:

> "I had wanted to belong to you, but you didn't want it. You are so self-sufficient there is hardly any place for me in your life—except perhaps as a mistress." She added with a short laugh, "Babu, on the other hand, was on the edge of a breakdown—and still is, for that matter. He needs me and what's more he says so. He loves me more than he loves himself—that's more than can be said for you. In return, I am prepared to give him all that I have." (160)

Sindi is isolated, alienated and atomised because of the ambiguity in his approach towards the moral predicates of the *Gita*. He had led a life of voluptuous indulgence. At some crucial point, he gets fed up and diverts his attention towards detachment. But as soon as June comes into his life, his theory of detachment crumbles down. His attitude towards sex assumes an ambivalent character. Sindi suffers because he can neither control his desires nor transform himself by transcending the narrow boundaries of egoism. His desires, passions, anger and fear weaken him. The philosophy of detachment imposed from outside without purging the inner self of the pleasures of sense objects, confuses him further. Sindi learns, after much suffering, that he could get at the roots of detachment only by assuming responsibility and by developing perception of the unity of cosmic life. After June's death, he reflects:

> Detachment at that time had meant inaction. Now I had begun to see the fallacy in it. Detachment consisted of right action and not escape from it. The gods had set a heavy price to teach me just that. (192)

In India he meets the family members of Babu. Mr. Khemka, Babu's father is a business tycoon whose only aim is unscrupulous amassing of wealth? Mr. Khemka offers Sindi a job in his firm but a fresh crisis comes in the life of Sindi. The Income Tax people raid Khemka's office and his house; consequently Khemka is jailed on charges of forgery. Sindi then walks out and searches a new job in Bombay. But before his departure, he goes to the house of Muthu, who is a low paid employee in Khemka's office. Muthu lives in one roomed tenement with a dozen other people. Sindi is deeply touched by the squalor of the place and the wretchedness of Muthu's lot. Muthu makes an impassioned plea to Sindi to take charge of Khemka's business and save him and others like him from starvation. Sindi did not want to get involved but Muthu convinces him that 'sometimes detachment lies in actually getting involved.' (225) Sindi thereupon takes over the office and with the willing co-operation of the staff brings to effect several economic policies and sets all kinds of wheels in action with the result that the business soon picks up. The cynical exponent of non-involvement becomes overnight, as it were, a warm-hearted and purposeful man of action.

Sindi Oberoi is akin to existential heroes like Meursault in representing the present crisis of man, the absurdity of situation, the human struggle against nothingness, but he differs with them in his latent human element, his inner urge and restless quest for peace. Sindi has an ancestry; he inherits a genetic mystic drive. Right from the beginning he had a thirst: "I wanted to know the meaning of my life." (167) London classroom teaching hardly reveals anything to him. He works as a dish-washer in a hotel, comes in contact with Anna, Kathy and June, makes enormous reading in Scotland village library, and discusses God and mysticism with the priest. In course of his walk one day, he climbs a hill and sits on a weathered stone, where, in a flash he comes to understand that all love is illusion and illusion is the root of pain. Babu and June's deaths stun him but his urge for quest still solved some of the questions my existence had posed for me; but persists: "one thing was certain: my search had to continue. I had many more remained to be solved." (175) in fact, June's death acts as a tragic peripetia. He gets another flash of insight at the river where he goes after June's death and watches the dawn breaking over the dark water and the sun rising. Detachment at that time had meant inaction. Now, he had begun to see the fallacy in it. Detachment consisted of right action and not an escape from it. The primordial symbols of hill, river and sun indicate that Sindi is on the right path of becoming. The dawn breaking the dark water is the breaking of the darkness within him. Consequently, when he comes to India, he encounters at Khemka's house, the bronze figure of dancing Shiva. He is held, as it were, in supreme ecstasy:

> For a moment, just one brief moment, I was struck by the intense beauty of the divine dancer. America. India, Egypt, all mingled behind him in aeons of increasing rhythm. (11)

The archetypal image of the dancing Shiva is a product of Arun Joshi's collective unconsciousness, his racial inheritance, his Indian heritage. It is also a correlate to the turning phase in Arun Joshi's odyssey in life. The protagonist is a quester incognito. This image gets fuller dimension in the symbol of Lord Krishna that pervades the whole of *The Last Labyrinth*. The dancing Shiva is the paradox of truth; he is both destructive fury and creative force. Sindi Oberoi has been passing through a process of death and a new man is now born as it were. In the beginning, his experiences in India are obviously not much different from those in the West. Only the theatre has changed, the show continues. But gradually Sindi Oberoi's understanding deepens as he roots himself into the world of the miserable that live in rags. Human suffering purges him, awakens him to the real meaning of detachment. When Mr.

Khemka's industry is ruined, Sindi decides to leave for Bombay. On the morning of departure, the first monsoon shower comes. The shower is fertility symbol, signaling the stirring of life in Sindi also. That afternoon when the sky is clear, he goes to meet Muthu. The clear sky signals full light of knowledge that will dawn upon Sindi. In Scotland the hill had whispered something to his soul, in Boston the river, in India Muthu becomes the human voice of the divine truth. What has been dangling before Sindi earlier, now turns washed in daylight. He understands finally that detachment does not mean escape or alienation, it means involvement, devotion, sacrifice. Muthu is a human carrier of the message of the *Gita*. Sindi takes over the management of the imprisoned Khemka's business and is fully devoted to the task of carrying the sinking ship of Surindra. He has learnt the secret of non-attached action of the *Gita*: ""Karmanya vadhika raste maa phalesu kadachana" Genuine detachment means Sthitapragya.

The novel in its final implication is a bitter indictment of both the assertion of alienation and the distorted concept of detachment or renunciation. The existential dilemma, the anguish of alienation and the absurdity of situation never remain the final predicament. Arun Joshi's central motif is quest and the characters are pilgrims in this sense. They combine both Malamud's Yokov Bok's search for the human and Kafka's K's search for God.

Arun Joshi's *The Last Labyrinth* bristles with modern sensibility. In the garb of the tormented hero, Som Bhaskar, the novelist explores the human psyche in all its subtleties in the modern context, when man is saddened by opposite forces and struggles hard to get out of the rut but feels confounded and is unable to choose his way. The word "Last" prefixed to "Labyrinth" denotes "death" which is the ultimate destiny of modern man. Confused, a prey to morbidity, put in a whirlpool of circumstances, he is ultimately destroyed.

The Last Labyrinth imparts fresher perspectives on the earlier novels because apart from carrying their genesis it explores the anguish of alienation and the intensity of quest with great force and complexity. The opposing worlds of science and religion, doubt and faith, East and West, Darwin and Krishna find congruent fictional articulation through the juxtaposition of paradoxical symbols and pervasive image of the Labyrinth. The characters of Som's mother, Anuradha, Gargi and the symbolic, mystical nuances of Krishna, the blue flame and the God latent in every particle of nature and surroundings in the hills create a backdrop which emerges as more emphatic and appealing in comparison to Som's restlessness and Leela Sabnis' Descartean analysis of everything.

Sternly suppressing sentimentality, Arun Joshi represents an unvarnished picture of life, laying special emphasis on the forces that make for the frustration of the individual, whether they spring from human passions or are occasioned by the working of society.

The Last Labyrinth tells the story of a man with morbid lack of belief in himself. It is a grim book in which the working of circumstances has a menacing inevitability. The total effect is, however, not depressing; rather the novel lays bare the modern sensibility and the interplay of doubt and belief, reason and dogma, faith and spirit, science and religion. The plot is firmly knit, the characters well-drawn and seen from the outside in the round as well as realised emotionally from within.

Som Bhaskar, the hero of the novel, is young, educated, intelligent millionaire industrialist who reflects; "Hunger of the body. . . . Hunger of the spirit. You suffer from one or other or both."[5] Bhaskar is a modern anti-hero, embodying chaos and uncertainty. He possesses a Pascalian passion to know and perhaps to believe, but he cannot believe, and torn by doubts he walks tight-rope between life and death, illusion and reality, body and spirit. He suffers from an indefinable hunger, restlessness, a Hamlet-like incertitude, an inherent sickness. All his life he has sung the strident song: "I want, I want." (78) Shuttling between Bombay and Benaras, he is the product of the life that seems to have grown "indefinitely vast,"[6] to use Karl Jaspers' words. Denied the cohesive 'interlinkage' he goes for a desperate living, clinging to one object or person, fanning this passion or that, but he is never at peace with himself. Years back inside the cave of Ajanta, a peculiar experience of voids had seized him:

> It was cool inside and dark. Then the walls started to float in, trembling, shimmering, daubed here and there with colour. The colours

> were faint, as they are in dreams. I had stood there trying to make sense out of them. And then, as gradually as they had materialized, the walls dissolved into the darkness. I continued to stand there until I was cooler. The walls came and went in dizzy waves, the daubs of colour dancing before my eyes. The spasms of darkness grew steadily longer—or, so it had seemed. Finally, I could not stand it any longer. When the wall disappeared once again I dashed out. (47)

Som flits from one pleasure to another; he becomes the incarnation of the quest of hunger for the joy of life. He, therefore, goes in search of new experiences whether they concern business or fascination. Som mistakes his hunger as for sex and hence indulges in escapades with several women. But ironically, far from attaining a sense of fulfillment, he has a terrible sense of emptiness, of voids within and voids without. Not knowing what it is he desires, is in some ways a facsimile of Saul Bellow's Henderson. But his search does not take him to a merely old Africa but to an infinitely mysterious Benaras. He gets fascinated by an obsolete world decaying, yet urbane—the world of Anuradha and Aftab—and by the labyrinth of the haveli they inhabit.

The major incidents of the novel take place in the city of Benaras though the scene often shifts to Delhi and Bombay. While Anuradha and Aftab come from Benaras, Som comes from Bombay. There is something very mysterious about Lal Haveli—the dwelling place of Aftab amidst the labyrinth of Benaras. It is a house "built either with no plan or with a most meticulous plan." (34) The novelist gives a picturesque description of Lal Haveli.

> Perhaps, the entire haveli had been built as a maze. What an idea! . . In this place anything could happen. . . . It is all run down now, this haveli, but its labyrinth remains. (35)

The description of Lal Haveli reminds us of the haunted castle described by Horace Walpole in his novel, *The Castle of Otranto* minus its supernatural setting and the horror attached to it. Lal Haveli is, however, a mysterious building. It has rooms within rooms; corridors that only bring one back to where one started. It is a "Bhulbhulaiya" like construction with death as the "Last Labyrinth." The labyrinthine construction of Lal Haveli with its dangerous curves and turns haunts our memory from the beginning to the end of the novel. The word 'labyrinth' is intended to cover wide implications. It connotes the mysteries of life and death, soul and God, matter and spirit and above all existence and non-existence. Like 'Egdon Heath' in Hardy's *The Return* of *the Native*, Lal Haveli has a domineering influence. It is symbolic of the doom of man.

Som Bhaskar goes to Delhi in connection with business. He meets Aftab in a hotel. He is in a hot haste. The novelist puts down his feelings in the following words:

> There is a memory of a warm Delhi night. Inside the great hotel Aftab, goggled, in a maroon jacket, had held a reception for the plastic manufactures' Association, I had come only to talk of business. I was in a hurry. I was always in a hurry then, like a hare chased by unseen hounds. (12)

It is at this time that he happens to meet Anuradha. Anuradha, the mistress of Lal haveli, has mercury-like quality. There is something very mysterious about her nature, character and disposition. When Som looks at Anuradha in Delhi for the first time, Anuradha appears to him not only 'not clever' but also something like a "monument: tall, handsome, and ruined." (192) Som's love for Anuradha is peculiar, the more he looks at her the more he wants her. It is quite at late stage that Som learns from the family doctor 'K' about the antecedents of Anuradha. But now it is too late. The novel presents a spectacle of Som's progressive disillusionment. K.R. Srinivasa Iyengar observes: "*The Last Labyrinth* is the story of Som's misadventure with his dark and terrible love."[7] Som's passions for Anuradha, his pursuit of her is so intense that his adventure may well be defined as a misadventure.

The symbol of labyrinth—meaning number of paths and passages through which it is difficult to find one's way—is suggestive enough. It is not only applicable to the old maze like Lal Haveli. It is also applicable to Som and Anuradha's misplaced love. Besides, it also concerns the perplexing question relating to life, death, God, Soul and the first cause. The novel touches the existential question of the origin and transience of life and death. It also conveys the very fusion of the spiritual and the sensual which transforms things into objects for our consideration.

The novelist has no respect for accepted conventions and he subjects them to a withering scrutiny. Values that are not susceptible of scientific proof he rates as fictitious. Consequently, untouched by sentiment, he finds himself able to reject much that has hitherto been considered sacred and part of our cultural inheritance.

The novel begins with Som Bhaskar's self-analysis of his unusual existence from what he says about himself. His education has been splendid. He is proud of having received education at Harvard University in America. He is a millionaire at the age of twenty five. He, however, hates money. He perpetuates noble thoughts. In Som's own words;

> I had been to the world's finest universities or what were supposed to be such. According to Mr. Thapar, who kept account of such things, a quarter million had been spent on my education. And there were things that I had picked up by myself. I knew that money was dirt, a whore. So were houses, cars, carpets. I knew of Krishna, of the lines he had spoken, of Buddha at Sarnath, under the full moon of July, setting in motion the wheel of Righteousness of Pascal, on which I did a par at Harvard. (11)

Som is broken, depressed, hysterical and adroit. He considers himself a nuisance "to 'K,' to Geeta, to myself." (10) Som's father dies of heart attack, when Som was hardly twenty five. He is married to his choice girl Geeta whom he calls, "an extra-ordinary woman' and is a father of two children. He is an intellectual with a scientific bent of mind. He believes in the triumph of human reason over the instincts of the blood. He deals with conflicts and soul-storms of sex on an almost epic scale. He is born and brought up in India but studies abroad. His father being a scientist always tries to unravel the mystery of creation of universe:

> Who knows the truth? Who can tell where and how arose the universe. The gods are later than its beginning: who knows, therefore, whence comes this creation? Only that God who sees in highest heaven: He only knows whence came this universe. He only knows. Or, perhaps he knows not. (155)

Som's mother is a very religious woman and has full faith in God, her Krishna. She is dying of cancer but she refuses to take pills because she believes Krishna would cure her. She dies of cancer. Som inherits Krishna from his mother. He has abiding love for Krishna. There is conflict within him because of two inherent forces—science and religion.

The intermingling of different forces makes Som Bhaskar a psychological case. He loses his mother at an early age of fifteen. He feels insecure. Som experiences a terrible void when he visits Ajanta at the age of eighteen. From what he feels at that moment it is clear that he believed in the evanescence of all material objects including life. Life is fleeting to him. Nothing appears stable. This feeling persists in his life all through. He always remains in a state of confusion. He is incapable of distinguishing between right and wrong. The hollowness and restlessness of Som is not like that of Billy and Sindi. The life of Billy is estranged and he feels that he is not authenticated in the commercial and money-conscious civilization. But Som has no problem with the society. He is not an alien in the commercial world of Bombay. His inflictions are internal. These qualities make Som emotionally a labyrinth. He is torn by the inner contradictions and his consciousness wanders in the maze of the opposite impulses. He suffers from an intense feeling of inadequacy, a feeling of rootlessness and a feeling of rudderless boat being tossed on turbulent waves. He accepts:

> If only one knew what one wanted, or, maybe, to know was what I wanted. To know, just that. No more, No less. This then, was a labyrinth, too, this going forward and backward and sideways of the mind. (53)

Som rushes to the arms of innumerable women to forget the sense of insecurity and in search of a nucleus. But every time he is repelled with greater force and the voids come upon him. The increased number of relationships does not decrease his discontentment. He is attracted towards Leela Sabnis with more intensity and vigour than others. Leela Sabnis is an explorer, trained in Michigan in the tools of exploring. Her contention is apparent regarding the world of reason and mysteries. Som being a disillusioned man feels dissatisfied with her stance. The conversation between Leela Sabnis and Som throws sufficient light on the temperaments of both.

> Leela Sabnis had obsessions. She had an obsession for explanations. Like my father. What led to what? Causes and effects. Effects and effects. What made people tick. The neat kingdoms of reason.
>
> "I am not fond of you," she told me one evening. "That would be lying, but I am concerned, I am worried. Tell me, what makes you tick?"
>
> "The voids," I said without enthusiasm.
>
> "The voids? What voids?"
>
> "I hear this song way up in the sky. All the time."
>
> "What song?"
>
> "I want, I want, I want, I want, I want, I want."
>
> "Just like that?"
>
> "Yes." (78)

Apparently, while Leela Sabnis is inclined towards concrete and tangible, Som is inclined towards abstract and intangible. When Leela Sabnis asks him as to what makes him behave in a particular manner, he replies that he cannot tell it with certainty as he sees nothing before him except impenetrable void. His every bit of action is motivated by the inner urge, 'I want.' He wants and wants are unlimited. Consequently, he floats in the void. His position may be likened to that of the Hollow men described by T.S. Eliot.

> Between the desire
> and the spasm
> between the Potency
> and the existence
> between the essence
> and the descent
> falls the shadow.[8]

The hunger of Som is of body and soul both. Som's affair with Leela fizzles out within six months.

At the age of thirty-five, he visits Delhi in order to participate in a reception function organized by Aftab for the plastic manufacturers. Aftab calls on him in the luxurious international hotel where the latter is putting up. It is for the first time that Som is introduced to Anuradha. But his acquaintance with Anuradha is not complete until she invites him to Benaras and Amzad Mian takes him to the Dargah. Aftab's character is portrayed in vivid colours. He is a highly romantic man. Aftab unquestionably comes of a re-

spectable family. His great grandfather was a Zamindar and a courtier of Wajid Ali Shah, the nawab of Lucknow. The family shifted to Benaras after the mutiny. Amzad Mian, old and grey-haired, is a great votary of God and religion. He frequently quotes Islamic scriptures. When Aftab, Som and Anuradha accompany Amzad Mian to the Dargah, it is he who dilates upon the perishable body, the fana. It is at the Dargah that Som develops intimacy with Anuradha. This intimacy flowers into love. This love is not the unusual love between the lover and the beloved but the love that brings pain and disaster.

Gargi occupies a pivotal position in the novel. She lives on the bank of Ganga in Benaras in her small cottage. She is the daughter of a Sufi—a Peer. Gargi's character is assessed at the face value. Som often opens his heart to Gargi. Som is torn by the conflict between faith and doubt. Because of his innate habit, he resists and argues at every step. He tries to have faith but there is always a mark of interrogation in his mind, which resists and stops him to accept anything blindly. He accepts his fault and confides to Gargi, "I want to assure you I am not vain. I am not arrogant. I am curious. I want to know. Maybe over-curious but not vain." (214) In this quest, Bhaskar wrecks himself. Thus, he starts to neglect his health, business and sanity and succumbs to melancholia as 'K' diagnoses. Gargi lays emphasis on suffering. She tells Som that God will send someone to help him: 'Someone who has known suffering.' (118) Gargi has unflinching faith in God's benevolence. Som doubts the existence of God. But he endorses the views of Gargi that God is all-pervasive and all-powerful. "Prayer does not change God. Kierkegaard had said, "but it changes him who prays. Maybe, I ought to start attending temples every evening." (118) Inheriting her father's urge and emulating him, Gargi has realized the presence of God. Her touch works as a healing balm on ailing Aftab. Joshi employs her as a symbol of living proof of God's presence.

Aftab is an important business man. Som first meets Aftab with the intention of buying his shares as he considers Aftab a 'tycoon.' But from the day he comes in contact with Anuradha, his interest shifts from Aftab's business to Anuradha. Anuradha becomes his main obsession. Ever since Som comes in contact with Anuradha at the Dargah, he feels attracted towards her. Anuradha appears to him like a woman one sees in Mughal 'miniatures.' He is drawn towards her, as it were, by a strong magnetic pull. When Som asks Anuradha to leave Aftab alone because he is no match for her, she tacitly admits it. This is enough for Som to think that Anuradha likes him.

Anuradha has witnessed many ups and downs in her life. Aftab acknowledges her acute suffering. Dr. Kashyap also knows much about her. She has passed through the different stages of suffering. Suffering has purged her soul. The prolonged suffering has taught her to circulate the milk of human kindness to all. Aftab tells Som, "It is just that she can't stand to see anybody fail. It breaks her heart." (39) She believes in *Vasudhaiv kutumbkam*. That is why she loves one and all. She has neither detached Aftab nor Som. She sleeps with Som but lives with Aftab in Haveli. Referring to Aftab, Som puts a question to Anuradha. "But are you his?" Anuradha replies, "Am I not?" Som puts another question, "You don't sound certain." To this question she replies, "I am not certain." Som is now of the view, "If she was not Aftab's, nor, perhaps, was she mine." (125) When he raises the question of fidelity, she replies that she has never been unfaithful. In the beginning, Som is under the impression that Anuradha must be the wife of Aftab with whom she has been living in Lal Haveli. But he is taken aback to know from the horse's mouth:

> "Married?" She laughed. "I have never been married,"
> For a moment I was too confused to speak.
> "Aren't you and Aftab married?"
> "Of course not. I just live with him."
> "I see." (43)

She is not married to anyone nor does she intend to do so because of her feeling: "You cannot marry everyone you love. Som wl y marry anyone at all?" (43) When Som asks her if she would like to be married to someone, she says; "I can imagine I am married to Aftab. I can imagine I am married to you. My mother used to imagine she was married to Krishna." (128)

Som gets puzzled at the statement of Anuradha. From what she says about herself, he thinks that she is no more than a chameleon harlot. But after a second thought, Som is convinced that Anuradha's chastity is unquestionable. He now understands the broad-heartedness of Anuradha. He develops infatuation for her despite the revelation about her character in the hope to get her sooner or later. This hallucination drives him nowhere. Anuradha accepts Som's proposal and offers him her body in spite of her disinterest in the physical pleasure. She sacrifices not for a sensual pleasure but she attempts to inspire joy in others. She has liberated shame, fear and sensual urge. Her sacrifice suggests her attainment of the cosmic vision. She is next to Gargi. She identifies herself with Krishna on the Janmashtami day, with the lepers, the beggars and with Gargi. Anuradha is following the footprints of Gargi and she is almost on the verge of attainment of enlightenment. Som feels the sympathetic vibration received from Anuradha down in his artery. Som describes:

> There was a mystery about Anuradha that I had yet to crack. She should have been no more to me than a woman trying to save her lover's (husband's?) property. She should have been transparent. Why should she appear mysterious unless, possibly, there was a mystery within me that, in her proximity, got somehow stirred, as one cunning fork might stir another. (89)

Therefore, for sometime, Som is stirred by the vibrations of Anuradha. Gargi of course represents Anuradha as Som's Shakti;

> She pulled out her slim little pad and passed me a note. 'Go with her,' it said. 'Don't quarrel. She is your *Shakti.*' To this day, I do not know what Gargi meant by that. But Anuradha, I learnt that night, was indispensable to me. (121)

She is the embodiment of power who leads Som to salvation. She is intimate to Som but this relationship is not based on passion. She decides to leave Som if he returns from the door of death. Som tries to snatch her away but she makes a supreme sacrifice by disappearing from Lal Haveli.

This world is mysterious and meandering because of the inhabitants like Gargi, Aftab and Anuradha. For Som this world is a mystery, a labyrinth since he has not suffered. He does not know sorrow. He has not developed large-heartedness like Gargi, Anuradha and Aftab. Aftab once tells him:

> You don't understand us. You work by logic. By your brain. You are proud of your education or what you consider education. There is an understanding that only suffering and humiliation bring. Anuradha has that. Even I have a bit of it. You are empty of that understanding. (217)

Som dislikes Aftab, Lal Haveli and Benares. The communication of Som with Anuradha, Gargi and Aftab is only possible, if he suffers. He accepts the difference between him and Geeta:

> If discontent is my trademark, trust is Geeta's. She is an intelligent person, sophisticated, aware of the pitfalls of the world. Why then this trust in the world's mechanisms, this faith that the engine shall not seize, or worse, explode. (63)

There is a conflict between the 'discontent' and 'trust.' He leaves Leela Sabnis because she cannot co-operate with him in his quest for wisdom. She lacks wisdom because she has not passed through 'sorrow and suffering.' Som leaves the world of reason, luxury, sensuality and sophistication, the world where mind grows and heart withers. Som is trying to achieve the perfection of his soul. He yearns for Anuradha, his soul. He seeks Gargi's help. She assures him and says, "We are all children trying to reach up to a crack in the door to peep into a room." (214) The metamorphosis of Som's soul is in progress. The dirt and filth clouding the vision are being cleaned by his sufferings. Som has started his effort to attain realization and to level up the perfection at par with Gargi and Anuradha. Gradually he develops the earlier stage of ignorance. The early Som doubts the existence of God but now there is no doubt. Doubt has been replaced by faith. Now, he is a changed person. He is sincere, serious and tries to confirm the existence of God. He himself wonders at the change in his motive. Once he had desired to purchase the share of Aftab's company and to possess Anuradha as his private property:

> I had started off that evening at the Intercontinental by grabbing at Aftab's company and here we are. There must surely be some truth that connects the two. (139)

His growth is apparent. He exposes his doubt to Gargi, Anuradha and Aftab:

> The point is that this Spirit is there and if it is there, if man has inherited it, then what is he to do with it? In other words, what precisely is expected of him, of you and me, of Anuradha, of everyone else? Darwin didn't say how we are supposed to evolve further. (132)

They try to satisfy his query. Aftab suggests that vision is demanded. The spirit also requires the visions of God. Anuradha also tries to convince him that Darwin is not the ultimate reality. She tells him, "Maybe Krishna begins where Darwin left off." (132) This remark surprises Som. In spite of his development until this moment, he does not succeed in reaching the bottom of the ocean like Anuradha. Som leaves his world of industry to encounter Krishna. He goes to the mountain to have an evidence of the existence of God.

Som has an unusual dream. He dreams that he is flying amidst mountains. He has this dream off and on since he fell ill. He narrates his dream before K: "It is something about flying or so it always happened. I am flying towards mountains, with a snow covered peak." (159) Sigmund Freud, in his dream analysis, has propounded the theory of wish fulfillments. Suppressed desires find outlet in dreams. Som is vexed with his living. He wants relief. He can get relief only in the world of spirits. God is his last solace. His life is made up of questioning. Upto now, he has been oscillating between two extremes 'Yes' and 'No.' This confusion, this dilemma, this fruitless quest has literally destroyed him. The fatal blow came when Anuradha also slips away from his hands. The loss of Anuradha compels him to realize his limitations. God has punished him. He has got the lesson that the path of confrontation does not lead to perfection. Now it is only God who can liberate him from weariness and doubts. Som's dilemma is a typical representation of an Indian with a Western orientation and education.

The novel ends on a note of Som's anguish and frustration. Aftab and Som are rivals in love for Anuradha. One night Som dreams that somebody is whispering to him that Aftab is dead. Just then, he feels that Aftab's corpse stretched out his hand and caught him by his wrist. He wakes up shaken. Before this gruesome incident, Som receives an unstamped and unsigned letter addressed to him apparently written by Aftab. Aftab opens his heart in his letter.

> For me now, he writes, 'all is desolation . . . take hold,' I tell myself. . . . 'Take hold Aftab Rai, you can live without her.' . . . 'But I cannot live without her . . . endlessly, I walk the mazes . . . night turns into day . . . day into night. . . . I knock my head against walls . . . cry cut my love for her . . . she does not listen. . . . I am finished . . . I had liked you. . . . I had let a snake enter my home . . . she thought she would handle you . . . She came that night from Bombay and said you were dying . . . The secret of her love written on her face. I was happy you were dying. . . . She went across the river . . . spoke of the night many years ago . . . when she out her wrist . . . told me you will never . . . never put your treacherous foot in Lal Haveli. . . . But I know . . . she knew. . . . If she was proven wrong . . . if you even returned . . . you would pay heavily . . . why you returned? . . . How I hate you . . . curse you . . . you escaped to the hotel that night . . . but how long. . . . Your time will come. . . . While you live you will rot . . . when dead you shall not find peace. . . . from one graveyard to another you will wander . . . a million years. (222)

Som Bhaskar's dream and the unstamped and unsigned letter he receives from Aftab reveal how much mentally disturbed he is. Aftab hated him because he is his new rival in love and he looks upon him as a snake who has been mistakenly allowed to touch the precincts of Lal Haveli. Aftab has been long in the look out to liquidate him but somehow or other he escaped. He warns Bhaskar that in case he dares to visit Lal Haveli again, he will have to pay heavily for it, meaning, he may have to lose his life. Aftab expresses his inmost feeling that he cannot live without Anuradha. He curses Bhaskar for betraying her. He tells him that peace will be denied to him even after he is no more. He would wander from this graveyard to that in search of peace for a million years. Bhaskar's agony knows no bounds. His long travail in quest of pleasure ultimately turns futile. His craving is something like running after a mirage.

That the novelist is influenced by the Western thought as also by the Indian philosophy is quite obvious from this novel. Bhaskar struggles in his life with the help of the teachings of the *Gita*: "Bhaskar's dilemma takes full cognizance of the post-*Nietzschean* Western world where God is dead and the Indian life suffused with the teachings of Krishna in the *Bhagwad Gita* that He is everywhere in everything. The presence of Krishna in the mother's room, in the human forms of the dancing pair on Janmashtami Day in Benaras, in the mountains, in the blue flame burning since ages, is an implicit demonstration of the essence of Indian spiritual heritage that the Atman (Brahma, God) is in every atom."[9]

The dilemma of Bhaskar represents an example of the mixing up of the Western and Indian ethos. As a matter of fact, Som finds himself lost in the labyrinth. The absurdity of Bhaskar isn't like Camus' Meursault. He is not unconscious of the incidents occurring around him. His curiosity is not defunct. He inquires and tries to know everything. The disappearance of Anuradha makes him insane. He rants:

> Anuradha listen. Listen to me wherever you are. Is there a God where you are? Have you met Him? Does He have a face? Does He speak? Does He hear? Does He understand the language that we speak? Anuradha, if there is a God and if you have met Him and if He is willing to listen, then, Anuradha, my soul, tell Him, tell this God, to have mercy upon me. Tell Him I am weary. Of so many fears; so much doubting. Of this dark earth and these empty heavens.

Till the end, such strange, mad thoughts impinge on him and he does not know if they are harbingers, the pilot escort, of melancholia or insanity or Faith. He is not merely a twentieth-century Hamlet transfixed between to be or not to be but adds to his dilemma to believe or not to believe. He may be compared with Abhimanyu in the *Mahabharata* who is not able to come out of the Chakravyuha. Bhaskar loses himself in the labyrinths of life and death, reality and truth, doubts and faith. In his quest, in his intent to unravel the cosmic mystery, Bhaskar is like a modern Nachiketa who has been denied the faith and resolution of the Upanishadic model.

On the pattern of the eminent German novelist Kafka, Joshi dives deep into the personal life of Som Bhaskar who is completely lost in the maze of life. He is in a state of utter confusion, and bewilderment, much to the detriment of his belief and ideology. Kafka's novels are gloomy records of frustration. He depicts man as a puppet in a strange, dreamlike world, seeking to find his salvation but always caught in a nightmare tangle of adverse situation. Likewise, Bhaskar struggles for his existence. He is not fickle-minded nor does he fight shy of odd circumstances. But his ambition is thwarted every time. Like the protagonists of Kafka's novels *The Trial* (*Der Prozess*, 1925) and *The Castle* (*Des Schloss*, 1926), Bhaskar is not able to choose his right path. The path is so labyrinthine that he is apt to lose his way. Here the novelist's philosophy has much to do with the deterministic philosophy of the great German philosopher Nietzsche.

The existential dilemma assumes a metaphysical dimension in *The Last Labyrinth*. Arun Joshi has explored the life of the modern upper class urban Indian people. The dilemma of existence in the novels of Nayantara Sahgal and Anita Desai emerges from the broken human relationship and lack of emotional complex. In Arun Joshi, the roots do not lie in emotional dissonance but in the very condition of living. It is a metaphysical reality. What Samuel Becket has been doing in his absurdist plays, Joshi has done in this novel. Exemplifying as it does, the existential absurdity of man's situation, the novel forcefully describes the enigmatic predicament of Som Bhaskar common in modern time. The total human situation and the ultimate significance of human existence are explored. Unarguably *The Last Labyrinth* is a fictional ideogram of human existence.

Arun Joshi is no experimenter in technique as James Joyce is. He is content to use traditional form and plot although his conception of the dynamic of personality is peculiarly his own. He cast his characters in modern setting keeping in view the fact of changing human values. In *The Last Labyrinth*, the personality to be explored and re-created is that of a typical modern man. Som Bhaskar is on the threshold of middle age. Incidents of his life and the accompanying visuals, mental and emotional impressions are set down from moment to moment in the style of Dorothy Richardson with a touch of Kafka. The novelist is haunted by the chaos and disaster of modern life and he seeks solace in conventional values. But to his great frustration, he witnesses the conflict between materialism and the world of spiritual values. However, he gets nothing save unmitigated ennui and dejection. This precisely is the dilemma of existence of a modern man. Arun Joshi has brought to Indian English novel a fine objectivity. He observes man and life closely, especially man under adverse conditions, man in the grip of elemental fear. He has observed the processes of mental and moral decay and has watched attempts at regeneration foiled by inner weakness and betrayed by self-delusion.

NOTES

1. Arun Joshi, *The Foreigner* (Orient Paperbacks, New Delhi, 1968).
2. O.P. Bhatnagar, "Arun Joshi's *The Foreigner*: A Critique of East and West," *The Journal of Indian Writing in English*, 1973, pp. 13-14.
3. *Quest,* 60, January-March, 1969, p. 101.
4. Robert M. Mac Iver, *The Ramparts We Guard* (Macmillan, New York, 1950), p. 84.
5. Arun Joshi, *The Last Labyrinth* (Vision Books, New Delhi, 1981), p. 11.
6. Karl Jaspers, *Man in the Modern Age*, trans. Eien and Cedar Paul (New York, 1956), p. 202.
7. K.R. Srinivasa Iyengar, *Indian Writing in English* (Sterling, New Delhi, 1987), p. 748.
8. T.S. Eliot, 'The Hollow Men,' *Selected Poems* (Faber and Faber, London, 1975), p. 80.
9. H.M. Prasad, *Arun Joshi* (Arnold Heinemann, 1985), p. 105.

Looking beyond the Wide Waste
Kiran Desai's *The Inheritance of Loss*

Kiran Desai's first novel *Hullabaloo in the Guava Orchard* and *The Inheritance of Loss* are of great topical interest. Though the former does not directly deal with the theme of alienation, which is Kiran Desai's main concern in her second novel, *The Inheritance of Loss*, the seeds of alienation may be found intertwined in the structural design of her first novel in as much as it highlights the exploration of identity in a superstition-stricken world. The dialectics of blind faith and emancipation, of fanaticism and fake religiosity versus logic and reasoning is probed into through a story which is highly vivifying and titillating and sense provoking. Sampath Chawla's every bit of gesture provokes peals of laughter.

Hullabaloo in the Guava Orchard was published in 1998, for which she won 'Betty Trask' award. It was the novel which was highly applauded by Salman Rushdie. It is a satirical novel dealing with the clash between religious fanaticism and reasoning. The theme of this novel is not directly concerned with isolation or alienation. But the seeds of isolation and alienation may be found dormant in this novel which subsequently sprouted in her second much-talked of novel, *The Inheritance of Loss*.

It seems germane, first to see where does the interest of her first novel *Hullabaloo in the Guava Orchard* lie. The protagonist of this novel is Sampath Chawla., the son of elderly Mr. Chawla, a resident of Shahkot, a thickly populated town in Punjab State. The town has several bazaars, schools, government offices, banks and degree college. There is also a post office. Sampath works in the post office. He is highly romantic by nature. He is in the habit of tearing the envelopes addressed to other persons and reading them secretly in a clandestine manner. Letters with romantic contents especially are sources of great entertainment to him. But he dislikes his job. The work he does in the post office is repugnant to his taste and temperament. It is boring to him. He is tired of his dry, dull and tedious work. But how to get rid of this rut is a great problem to him. Once he participates in the marriage ceremony of his Boss's daughter. He behaves there wildly, much to the vexation of his boss. He is removed from his service. He is frustrated. But it is a God-sent boon to him in disguise. Although he has to face the rebuff of his father on this account, he is happy over his so-called emancipation.

One day he, just out of fun, moves to a guava orchard and climbs up a tree. People quickly congregate round the tree and try to dissuade him from jumping from this branch to that like a monkey. He poses to possess some mystic and spiritual power to know the personal life history of some onlooker. He even goes to the length of exposing personal details of the lives of some persons who are convinced of his inner sense. There is nothing wonderful about his behaviour for he has already gathered information about the people assembling there by reading their personal letters while he was posted as a clerk in the local post office. Amazingly enough, his words are taken as the words of a man endowed with supernatural power uttered in an inspired moment. He is lifted to the status of a 'Baba,' a 'Guru' and a 'Sanyasi.' Sampath's father exploits this situation. He propagates that his son is a godman and whatever he says is the word of God. This is his oblique design to earn money through the growing popularity of his son. Sampath becomes Monkey-Baba.

Sampath's every utterance has an aphoristic value. Once a lady asks him to find a remedy for her wayward son, Sampath says: "Add lemons to milk and it will grow sour." His answer to a question is always symbolic and suggestive which is in consonance with the mystic teaching of the ancient sages described in Indian scriptures.

There is an atheist who is deputed by an atheist society to make a threadbare enquiry into the activities of Monkey-Baba. He meets Sampath's mother, Kulfi, who goes to the nearby forest with a view to gathering spices and herbs. The atheist thinks that Sampath's mother must have mixed some intoxicant in his food and whatever Sampath says is under the toxic effect of the intoxicant. He takes down his finding. He goes to a tree above the massive cooking pot of Kulfi. It is a coincidence that when there is the final hullabaloo in the guava orchard, he falls into the boiling cooking pot. The pot is at once covered by Kulfi. This malady implies that whenever and wherever there is a tug of war between superstition, make-believe, fanaticism, religiosity and logic, reasoning and scientific thinking, usually the former triumph and the latter are boiled to death. Sampath is a burning example of this phenomenon. He befools so many intellectuals and dupes so many right-thinking people.

In course of time, actual monkeys infest the Guava Orchard and destroy the peace of the people living nearby. They climb up the trees, uproot the plants, cry violently and create havoc. Sampath's father, Mr. Chawla, wants to protect the guava orchard from the mischievous monkeys because it is the source of his revenue. Suddenly, a monkey protection society rushes in to save the animals as they are considered sacred in Hindu religion.

Kiran Desai hurls her cudgel at the age-long blind beliefs and ridicules the conventional habits of the Indian people. When a woman is in the family way, conjectures are made as to the male or female issue. The mother is "released happy and full of relief if the baby was a boy, released full of disappointment and resentment if it was not."

How Sampath Chawla is transformed from a desperate eccentric to a Monkey-Baba reminds us of R.K. Narayan's Raju in *The Guide*, who is a convict-turned-Mahatma. The rise and fall of Raju's fortune provides an excellent opportunity to R.K. Narayan to satirize the mentality of Indians. New wealth leads Raju to drinking and gambling. But there is a difference in the portrayal of the characters of Raju and Sampath Chawla. While circumstances force Raju to become a guide, circumstances force Sampath to become a hoax.

The main concern of Kiran Desai in *Hullabaloo in the Guava Orchard* is to satirize the instinctive weakness of the average Indian to take everything lightly without putting it to acid test. The result is that the so-called Babas are hoodwinking people and enjoying princely lives. They eat, drink and smoke at the cost of others pretending that they are messengers of God and they have spiritual power to predict the future of man and cure them of their fatal diseases. If somebody dares to incur their displeasure or else try to outrage their feelings, they are bound to reap bad consequences. Hardly there is a town or village in India which is free from this or that Baba. The matter reaches its climax when a Baba is detected as a veteran criminal involved in sex scandals or heinous crimes. The other side of the picture is all the more grotesque and gruesome. Some Babas, who are worth nothing clad in saffron dresses, are held in high esteem and are worshipped like Gods by high officials. Kiran Desai highlights the dialectics of such a mentality. The Monkey-Baba described in *Hullabaloo in the Guava Orchard* is a patient of paranoia, a psychological disease in which the patient is led by delusion that he is a representative of God and God speaks through him and he is above other persons and is capable of knowing past, present and future.

In the strictest sense of the term, this novel is not directly concerned with alienation but obviously it gives a hint at it. The Indians are groping in the dark. They are tied to taboos. Unless they break the tie of blind beliefs, superstition and taboos, they cannot realize their identities and without realizing their real selves, they would continue to be unknown of their own existence. Taking a cue from this seminal idea, Kiran Desai proceeds to write her second novel *The Inheritance of Loss* where she boldly voices the problem of alienation of the westernized Indians.

Kiran Desai's novel, *The Inheritance of Loss*, for which she was awarded Man Booker Prize in 2007, is a 'tour de force.' By writing this novel, Kiran stole a march on her mother, Anita Desai, the well-known Indian English novelist, who was thrice nominated for 'Man Booker Prize': *Clear Light of Day* in 1980, *In Custody* in 1984, and *Fasting, Feasting* in 1999. But the judges missed to see any spark in these works which might have merited the award. There is no denying the fact that Anita Desai has always remained a fountain of inspiration for her daughter. After toiling for eight years, Kiran got her second novel *The Inheritance of Loss* released in 2006 which was much talked of in the literary circles, arrested the attention of the discerning critics and when it was put to test by a panel of judges, it came out triumphantly and the judges unanimously declared it to be a masterpiece, a literary product par excellence. Kiran got the much-coveted award against her expectation. She got the award when she was 35. Prior to this, Arundhati Roy got the same award for her novel *The God of Small Things* in 1997, when she was 36.

Kiran dedicated her novel *The Inheritance of Loss* to her mother. "To my mother with so much love." When asked by Manoj Sharma, the correspondent of *Sahara Times* as to the role played by her mother in shaping the book, Kiran unhesitatingly replied: "When it came to this book, she was the only person who could understand what I was trying to do and what I was going through. She helped with the editing and in the end her opinion was that I had cut a little too much."[1] She records here debt of obligation to her mother for writing this novel: "I wrote this book so much in her company. I owe a debt so profound and so great that this book feels so much hers as it does mine."[2] Even the judges who evaluated the book observed: "I think her mother would be proud. It is clear to those of us who've read Anita Desai that Kiran has learned from her mother's work."[3] The award amounted to a tune of $ 93,000.

Born in New Delhi in 1971 to a German mother, Kiran spent her childhood in India and went to England when she was hardly 14 and then moved to United States where she stayed and received education. This enabled her to come in contact with multi-dimensional cultures of different countries and the social milieu of different people which helped her write on a broad canvas.

The Inheritance of Loss has many spectacular features, vivid characterization, well-knit and close packed plot, bewitching scenic setting, candid and graphic descriptions, unalloyed humour, scintillating and sparkling wit and, above all, a language and style which is Kiran's own. The book gives a sombre view of the post-colonial days, when the traditional Indian values were consigned to oblivion. Sometimes the novel has been over-praised and qualities have been assigned to it, just reverse of its literary merit. For example, Pankaj Mishra in a review of this book remarks: "Although, it focuses on the fate of a few powerless individuals, Kiran Desai's extraordinary new novel manages to explore with intimacy and insight, just about every contemporary international issue: globalization, multiculturalism, economic inequality, fundamentalism and terrorist violence. The reviewer overdoes the fact. What about racial discrimination, colour bias, religious bigotry and fanaticism, secularism and war-mongering? The novel does hint at globalization and terrorist violence. But what it has to do with fundamentalism—maintenance of traditional beliefs in opposition to modern dynamism? The novelist puts her philosophy in the mouth of Noni, which she by way of advice gives to Sai: "Don't go in for a life where time doesn't pass, the way I did. That is the single biggest bit of advice I can give you."[5]

Unquestionably, the novelist is opposed to nostalgia, the wistful longing to go back to the remote past without discrimination, for the past does not always contain everything worth having. The application of fundamentalism in her narrative is, therefore, out of question.

The novelist gives a fine spectacle of Kalimpong but it is not in accord with the changed situation in the 1980s. The novelist speaks of strikes, turmoil, lack of electricity, arrests, Gorkhaland campaign but all this was a worn-out legend in late 1980s. Thus she has presented "a lopsided picture of the locals and the place," (237-38) says Bharat Mani Pradhan, a Kalimpong-based social worker.[6] The novel also contains some obscene descriptions, which is not expected of a novelist, initially trained in aesthetic thinking. Two instances will substantiate this point.

The judge recollects his maiden romance with his wife Nimi. He is twenty and his wife is fourteen. "How he had half undressed and hurriedly redressed his wife, of how he had only glimpsed her expression, just bits and pieces of it in the slipping of her pallu over her head pleading but pompous." (38) The other description related to Nimi, who in order to flatter her husband, the judge, shows an unbecoming gesture: "She picked up the judge's powderpuff too grown up for children thieving, she knew, but she was filled with greed." (166) In the first quotation the imagery 'blind sea creature is patently obscene. Indisputably, it has sexual overtone. And this apart 'female flesh' in the context of a fourteen-year *Kishori* smacks of sexual perversion. The second quotation is equally fatuous. Here Nimi emerges as another Lady Chatterley. The style is reminiscent of Lawrence's minus his phallic philosophy.

The loss, the novelist observes in different spheres of Indian life, is appalling indeed. It is multifaceted. It concerns love-making, pecuniary implications, social status, self-aggrandizement, self-respect, righteousness and maintaining of indigenous qualities. Situation has come to such a pass that it has become almost impossible for a westernized Indian to identify himself as an Indian. The situation has gone beyond redemption.

The story of the novel is spread over a period of about four decades from 1943, when Jemubhai Popat Lal Patel was wedded to Bela, who later became Nimi, to 1986, when Biju, the only son of Jemu's cook came back to his native land India, sentimentally injured, physically harassed, well-nigh a broken man. The plot of the novel is set against the background of Darjeeling and Kalimpong, the Himalayan town, chiefly inhabited by Nepalese, lepchas, Bhutias and Tibetans. The novel opens with the descriptions of a horrifying scene suggestive of political jingoism. A gang of Nepali teenagers in leather jackets and Khaki pants intrude upon Jemu in his dilapidated house in Kalimpong, terrorize the inmates of the house, intimidate the cook, seek obedience by threats, make the judge and the cook say "Jai Gorkhaland, I am a fool" and finally make off with the trunks, one painted "Mr. J.P. Patel. S. S. Strallnavert" and the other painted "Miss S. Mistry, St. Augustine Convent" leaving behind a trail of smoke emitted by the fire-arms. It reminds us of those panicky days when the entire northern India, particularly the hilly tracts, was put in hot water making life insecure.

The most absorbing character of the novel is Jemubhai Popat Lal Patel, a Patidar by caste, and ICS officer, who is a retired chief justice living with Sai, his maternal grand-daughter, her pet dog Mutt and his cook in his house named Cho Oyo in Kalimpong. The house was actually built by a Scotsman who went back to Aberdeen. The portrait of the judge has been satirically drawn. He is the worst victim of the loss of inheritance. His loss is irredeemable. The judge is a mixture of opposites. He is a torn soul. He is made a caricature by the novelist. He has completely forsaken his heritage. "He envied the English. He loathed Indians. He worked at being English with the passion of hatred and for what he would become, he would be despised by absolutely everyone. English and Indians, both." (119)

A westernized Indian is bound to be doomed not only because he hangs between two cultural traditions but also because he is mentally defunct. The ladies chuckle at him: "But 'Aha' laughed a sister who was listening carefully, 'we sent you abroad to become a gentleman and instead you have become a lady.'" Jemu's father breathes sigh of relief: "Our family honour is gone. We are lucky. Bomanbhai is dead, thank God. It's the scandal of the town."

"It was a mistake to send you away. You have become like a stranger to us." (306) The judge does not like his wife although formerly he was madly in love with her. How can he love an unlettered rustic coming from village Pilphit? After all, he is raised to the pedestal of an honourable judge. Those days are gone when he was poor and humble and was tagged to a village girl. He warns his wife: "Don't show your face outside. People might run from you screaming." By year's end, the dread they had for each other was so severe that it was as if they had tapped into a limitless bitterness carrying them beyond the parameters of what any individual is normally capable of feeling.

"Now Jemubhai wondered if he had killed his wife for the sake of false ideals, stolen her dignity, shamed his family, shamed hers, and turned into the embodiment of their humiliation." (308) He recalls the words of his mother. "Didn't his mother think of the inappropriateness of her gesture? Undignified love, Indian love, stinking, unaesthetic love." (308) The judge's pernicious philosophy is: "A human can be transformed into everything. It was possible to forget, and sometimes essential to do so." (308)

Nor is this all. He has been living with his cook for long. But there is no understanding between them. "The judge and his cook lived together for more years than they had been with anyone, practically in the same room, closer to each other than to any human being and nothing, zero, no understanding." (313) While coming back from Cambridge, he brings a jar of green shave, a hair-brush and a comb set in silver, pompom with a loop of silk in a round container of powder. He sips beef tea. He feels flattered when Mrs. Rice addresses him as 'James.' He is obsessed by his power and position. The novelist depicts the metamorphosis in his character with fine artistic strokes. His egotism is described when he makes a monogram of his name with 'JPP' carved on it. His transformation is complete when he becomes completely self-centred in Kalimpong and hates mixing with a commoner. Untrammelled by any consideration, he puts on a weird countenance. He loses touch with his own mother tongue. He reads *How to Speak Hindustani*. The perversities his nature is beset with, do not allow him to see things around him distinctly and recognize his own men and prize his own cultural heritage. He is "being mistaken for something he wasn't, a man of dignity." (119) Like other elderly people, "He seemed not to have travelled forward in time but far back." (33) The novelist looks beyond the wide waste and finds every particle of Indianness dwindling into nothingness, Indian values set at naught. The smothered spirit of a westernized Indian of which the judge is a symbol, loving England and English things is well brought out by the novelist.

Though the cook talks tall of his master, the irony is that Jemu was born in 1919 in a humble family of a peasant caste under a palm roof scuffling with rats at Pilphit, a small village, which was subsequently owned by Gaekward kings of Baroda and still later by the British. Jemu received his education at Bishop's college on a scholarship. His father earned by procuring false witnesses to give evidence in the court. His father bought a second hand Hercules bicycle for him for Rs. 35. It was just a coincidence that he left for Cambridge and returned from there as a member of ICS. But on his return to India, he completely forgot his humble past days of poverty and deprivation.

Though a large part of the novel is devoted to bringing out the angularities in the character of the judge, the main theme of the novel hinges around Gyan and Sai, the hero and heroine of the novel. Gyan and Sai are introduced relatively late in the story.

When the judge finds that Noni is not capable of teaching Math to Sai, he appoints Gyan to guide her in Math and Physics. At that time Sai had just reached the threshold of youth. She was sixteen. Gyan was twenty. Nomita alias Noni and Lolita alias Lola were sisters living in a cottage named Ami. When Lola's husband died of heart attack, Noni shifted with her widow sister. Lola's daughter Pixie was BBC press reporter at that time. Noni was appointed teacher by the judge to teach Sai. But soon it was discovered that she was not well up in Math and so the judge opted for Gyan to teach Math to Sai. When they became close to each other, they narrated their woeful stories to each other. Sai said that around 1961, a Soviet team of aeronautical and aviation experts came to India to select candidates for the purpose of sending them to space and luckily her father Mr. Mistry was selected and was sent to Moscow, leaving her behind, when she was six years old and was a school girl. But as ill luck would have it, her father died and she became an orphan. Jemu, being her maternal grandfather, maintained her but never called on her. She never met her maternal grandfather till 1957. Her mother was also disowned by the family in Gujarat. She met the cook, when she came to Kalimpong after completing her education in Dehradun seven years back. Though she was an English speaker, while the cook was a Hindi speaker, there was no communication gap between the two. Gyan was moved by the pathetic life history of Sai and said that his plight was no better than hers. In 1880, his ancestors left their village in Nepal and came to Darjeeling in search of work in a tea plantation. The Imperial army selected soldiers over the hills. His great-grandfather died in Mesopotamia, where Turkish bullet made a sieve on his heart leaving behind his wife and three sons. After the passing away of his great grand-father his elder son was appointed in the army, who too was killed in Burma during war operation between the British and the Japanese. Then his brother was taken in, who also lost his life in Italy. He recalled that his father taught in a tea plantation school beyond Darjeeling. In this way, his life is a vale of tears.

As time passes, the reciprocal love of Gyan and Sai begins to blossom. Sai addresses Gyan as 'Kaju' and Gyan addresses Sai as

'Kishmish.' (140) Both miss each other. The novelist describes the passionate love of Sai in the following words: "That night, Sai sat and stared into the mirror. Sitting across from Gyan, she had felt so acutely aware of her self." (74)

"Marooned during curfew, sick about Gyan, and sick with the desire to be desired, she still hoped for his return. She was bereft of her former skill of solitude. She waited, read *Wuthering Heights*." (250) "They played the game of courtship, reaching, retreating, teasing, fleeting—how delicious the pretence of objective study, miraculous, how it could eat up the hours." (125)

In a typical Lawrentian style, the novelist describes the delicate moment when they exchanged their kisses.

> "Kiss me!" he pleaded.
>
> 'No,' she said delighted and terrified. She closed her eyes and felt the terrified measure of his lips on hers—trying to match one's shape with the other. (125)

Despite sincere efforts from both the sides their love does not come to fruition. Gyan likes to possess Sai in her totality. "Gyan and Sai would have melted into each other like pats of butter—how difficult it was to cool and compose themselves back into their individual beings." (129)

When Sai puts the baffling question to the cook whether the judge ever loved his wife, the cook replies in affirmative and adds: "There are many ways of showing love, not just the way of the movies—which is all you know. You are a very foolish girl. The greatest love is love that's never shown." (87) The cook's norm of love lends support to Sai's platonic love. Her ideology is: "Love must surely reside in the gap between desire and fulfillment. Love was the ache, the anticipation, the retreat, everything around it but the emotion itself." (2-3)

Pitted against the anglophile judge, haughty, self-obsessed and submerged in western culture from top to toe is his cook who is every inch Indian. He is greatly disappointed when Jemu starts living in Kalimpong in an ordinary way. It is much shock for the cook because his father had always served white men only. But by and large, he is a credulous fellow. In the end he is beaten up by the judge, who holds him responsible for the death of his pet dog Mutt.

Biju, the cook's son, goes to United States and becomes a great admirer of the culture of the west. With an infectious zeal, he writes letters to his father praising everything that belongs to America. His friend Saeed's impression is: "Oh, the United States, it's a wonderful country. And its people are the most delightful in the world." (122) But with the passage of time, he feels the pranks of America. He bleeds. He cries out: "It was horrible what happened to Indians abroad and nobody knew but other Indians abroad." (138)

Biju's torment in America is unspeakable. He spends his second year at Pinocchio's Italian restaurant. For some time, he also works at Gandhi café. He wished he were young so that he might have thought of going back to his country. It is too late for him to march a retreat. In America, Biju finds Indians taking beef. With a heavy and agonized heart, Biju narrated his suffocation to his Muslim friends in America. Saeed refuses to eat a pig on the ground that he is first a Muslim, then a Zanzibari and then an American. Biju feels that his motherland is beckoning him to come back soon. At last, his ambition is fulfilled. But by that time, Kalimpong is put in hot water. Everywhere there is turmoil, unrest and complete breakdown of administration. No attempt is made by any authority to allay apprehensions, which build up an atmosphere of distrust and disharmony. Nothing, not even Indo-Nepal treaty, gives political leverage to the situation and alleviates the suffering of the innocent local public.

From the pattern and the design of the novel, it is apparent that it is intended to demean the westernized Indians and highlight their wounds. Apart from the judge and Biju, even Sai, the heroine of the novel, has been described as a ruined character because she is a westernized Indian "brought up by English nuns, an estranged Indian living in India." (210)

The secondary plot, the role of Gorkha Liberation Front (GNLF) and Gorkha Liberation Army (GLA), is spun out as an integral part of the main web of the story. Biju, when he comes back from America to India, feels he has been thrown from fire to the frying pan. India does not give him any solace.

The novelist creates effect by describing something which is unfamiliar, bizarre and grotesque. The long lists of western dishes simply cause irritation. Similarly the tenuous details of the physical posture of Sai (47) and the working of electronic supersonic space-speed machine (81) are simply exasperating.

Besides this, Kiran has the Dickensian habit to create a galaxy of characters which hang here and there like loose threads. What purpose do uncle Potty, Father Booty, Sister Caroline, Chetu and Motu, Mrs. Thondup, Mr. Iype, Jeev Saran, Mr. Lalkaka, Mr. Kakkar serve? They are unnecessary scaffolding created upon the main structure of the tale. Besides this, the tale told is a hackneyed one. The situation has now undergone a radical change. No Indian who now goes to England or United States or any other foreign country loses his moorings with his motherland. He is seldom wounded by the west. On the contrary, he imposes his own civilization and cultural heritage on the foreigners. As a result whereof thousands and thousands of British and American people come over to India for peace and lesson.

But what is remarkable is that the merit of the novel outweighs its defects. Kiran Desai is still very young. She is full of promise. She may fill the repertory of Indian English fiction with another yet superior work—who knows?

NOTES

1. Manoj Sharma, *Sahara Times*, Panorama, Oct. 7, 2006, p. 29
2. Vijay Dot, cited, *Hindustan Times*, Friday Oct. 13, 2006 (London, Oct. 12).
3. *Ibid.*
4. Pankaj Mishra, "Wounded by the West," Review of *The Inheritance of Loss*, Feb. 12, 2006
5. Kiran Desai, *The Inheritance of Loss (*Penguin, 2006), p. 93
6. *Hindustan Times*, Patna, Correspondent, Cited Darjeeling, Nov. 3, 2006, *Hindustan Times*, Sah, Nov, 4, 2006

Conclusion
From Alienation to Alleviation

> Behind her, in an alcove, stood a bronze figure of dancing Shiva. For a moment, just one brief moment, I was struck by the intense beauty of the divine dancer. America, India, Egypt, all mingled behind him in aeons of increasing rhythm.[1]

From my present study, Kamala Markandaya, Anita Desai, Arun Joshi and Kiran Desai emerge as significant Indian English novelists vitally interested in exposing the complexities of modern life as it is lived in urban society. Mediocrity of taste and interests has eroded family ties, giving birth to growing problems of broken home, divorce, abandoned children and crime within the house. The stress of the surrounding in social, political, cultural and technological term is also felt everywhere. These problems and many others have been mirrored in modern Indian literature wrapped in different languages. These problems also form warp and woof of Indian English novels, particularly the novels of Kamala Markandaya, Anita Desai and Arun Joshi. These three major Indian English novelists look at the problem of alienation from three different angles. The novels of Kamala Markandaya deal with cultural alienation while the novels of Anita Desai and Arun Joshi deal with the problems of psychic alienation and Existential alienation respectively. These novelists tackle other problems also in their novels but their main interest revolves round the problem of alienation as mentioned above.

As time is passing, the values of life—social, moral, cultural, personal, economic—are crumbling fast. The result is that a typical modern novelist cannot write in the way Dickens, Thackeray, Jane Austen, Anand, Raja Rao and Narayan used to write. Modern novelists are confronted with different problems as compared with the novelists of the preceding ages. Whether in India or abroad, the novelists have turned their ken to life as we live today in all its complexities and intricacies of alienation and aloofness. Feelings of the angst, often neurotic, anguish, futility and incommunication have made deep roots in the Western life as a result whereof much of modern western novel, has developed as an existential fable on man's life. In the fictional narratives of Dostoevsky, Camus, Kafka and Bellow and in the plays of O'Neill, Miller, Williams, Ionesco, Beckett and several other significant playwrights, the tenor of alienation finds recurrent articulation. The tortured protagonists are metaphors of the deep-rooted alienation in western life. The experience of exile or incommunication has not become the crux of our identity so far. In India also, life is no longer tranquil or wholesome particularly in the urban areas. The torments of incommunication are spreading their tentacles. Incommunication has become the cardinal experience of the life of a significant segment of Indian society. Kamala Markandaya, Anita Desai, Arun Joshi and Kiran Desai have in their major novels explored the variegated dimensions of this dilemma.

In *The Coffer Dams*, Kamala Markandaya jostles a throng of British and Indian characters into cross-cultural situations, ways of life and attitude of mind. Clinton is a typical representative of European technological civilization, who looks upon India as the vast sprawling enigma. He represents the ruthless efficiency of business-minded British engineers. The chief of the tribe symbolizes suffering and tension as well as underlying hope and faith of uprooted inhabitants of the hills. The novel explores the encounter between western modernism and primitive forces of India through a confrontation between groups of British and Indian characters. The British characters, by and large, take pride in keeping close to themselves—they do not want to forge any communication with the outsiders. Jackson remarks, "We like keeping ourselves to ourselves." (75) And on the other hand, the Indians too do not acknowledge the Europeans. The cleavage is clear enough.

In Kamala Markandaya's *The Nowhere Man*, Srinivas and Mrs. Pickering are metaphors of their cultures interacting with each other in the most human and intimate terms. In them and in their relationships, the East and the West meet and merge but not permanently. The message of the novelist is that the East and the West have begun to understand each other, have started probing into each other's heart, but they cannot remain together. There is an impassable gulf between the two. Two races and two cultures can never be fully assimilated. This situation of coming closer and yet living apart creates the identity of crisis. The story of Srinivas is a tragedy of an Indian living in England, who tries to assimilate himself into the fabric of British culture. He spends nearly two third of his life in England and feels at home in it. Young English men like Fred, Joe, Bill and Mike compel him to feel otherwise. Fred harasses Srinivas and forces him to realise that he has no right to live in this country. Srinivas considers himself an unwanted man and tells Mrs. Pickering, "It is time when one is made to feel unwanted and liable as a leper, to be ostracized further perhaps beyond the limit one can reasonably accept oneself." (75) He gets almost shocked when he realizes that he has no place to go if he leaves this country: "'Nowhere,' he said to himself and he scanned the pale anxious eyes which were regarding him for reasons that might drive him out, a nowhere man looking for a nowhere city." (75) Two scenes of existential loneliness and the lack of belongingness impinge upon him. His reflection makes the picture of his stark isolation clear. He asks himself what is the final result of trying to assimilate in a foreign culture for so many years:

> As alien, he replied, speaking for them, in the voice that—if somehow, suddenly he were to be capitulated among them now—they would use. An alien, whose manners, accounts, voice, syntax, bones, build, way of life—all of him—shrieked alien! (169)

In these two novels, alienation has emerged from clash of cultures. Life in the twentieth century is far more dynamic and receptive to the changes occurring in the world. No country can insulate itself against the flow of time and consequently multicultural experience is a necessary condition of human situation in almost every alive country. Markandaya has the prerogative of participating in the life of India as well as England. She has assimilated in herself the tension of dual cultures and therefore she has successfully built her novels around the theme of incommunication arising out of the conflicting forces of two cultures. *The Coffer Dams* and *The No-*

where Man emerge as eloquent illustrations of the crisis of cultural alienation. However, to believe that world culture is an impossible proposition is to go to one extreme on the one hand and to believe that world culture is feasible is to go to another extreme. Unquestionably there is a need to strike a balance between the two which will augur well for the future. In the relationship of Helen and Bashiam (*The Coffer Dams*), Srinivas and Mrs. Pickering, Laxman and Plat (*The Nowhere Man*) the two cultures, British and Indian merge. They understand each other and this is a heartening sign. But the question how far we have succeeded in achieving this kind of blending, crystallization and assimilation is a debatable one. Literature has played a vital role in bringing hearts together. We have now a broad-based literature in which one might see the whole world reflected. Hence, those who maintain that assimilation of different cultures is impossible either live in intellectual back water or look at the problem with jaundiced eyes. Many Indian intellectuals are given recognition in foreign countries and honoured with covetable rewards.

Sidney Finkelstain has defined alienation as a "psychological phenomenon, an internal conflict, a hostility felt towards something, seemingly outside one self." (289) For Erich Fromm, the term alienation means "mode of experience in which a person experienced himself an alien. He has become one might say, estranged from himself." (168) This experience of estrangement or alienation finds first major explication in *Cry, the Peacock*, the first novel written by Anita Desai. Maya, the heroine, has an intensely imaginative sensitivity which contra distinguishes her from hard-boiled husband Gautama. Her marriage with Gautama is a misalliance as Gautama is several years older than her. He is a successful lawyer who holds a more prudent attitude to life. At the root of Maya's psychic retrogation lies the disparity between the dispositions of the husband and the wife. Maya experiences the world through sense while Gautama looks around through reason and logic. The conflict can be explained at various levels, between the world of illusion and the world of intellectual detachment personified in myth. Gautama's destruction implies that treated against the powerful imaginative world of Maya a timid intellect oriented world cannot subsist. However, *Cry, the Peacock* which appears to be full of despair and nihilistic stuff is also an attempt to face life. Bipin Panigrahi and Vinay Kirpal in the article, "Individual and the Search for Self identity in *Cry, the Peacock*" rightly illustrate, "Anita Desai achieves the harmonious blend of content and form—a harmony between the 'whatness' and the 'howness' of things—And this is what the novelist seek to suggest. A harmony between 'What is life and how it is to be lived' forms the core of Anita Desai's fictional world in the novel." (193)

Som P. Sharma and K.N. Awasthi find a 'vindication of the feminine principle in *Cry, the Peacock*.' (166) Anita Desai's concern with family problems is thought-provoking indeed. She freely uses myth and legends to heighten the effect of the fictional narrative. She is equipped with keen insight which enables her to analyse psychic alienation in conjugal life in all its subtlety and truthfulness. Being a woman, she is in an advantageous position because she has the feminine instinct to distinguish between what is worth having and what is to be discarded in marital life. Unlike Hardy she is a subtle psychologist too because she conceives her characters on psychological plane. She seems to be interested in the anguish of woman in a disturbed family emanating from the temperamental incompatibility of the husband and the wife. The world of Gautama, Maya's husband, revolves around money, court, chamber and cigarettes while the world of Maya is a world of feelings and sensations. What Maya wants from her husband is denied to her and what she heartily abhors is showered upon her. Gautama is drab and dry, drowned over head to foot in philosophy and mental acrobatics. This obvious cleavage accounts for the shipwreck of the family accord. Anita Desai seems to be fully justified in holding that for a happy conjugal life, a synthesis between the attitudes of the husband and the wife is a necessary condition. The albino astrologer's prophecy reminds us of the three weird sisters' prophecy in Shakespeare's *Macbeth* and the prophecy in Sophocles' *Oedipus Rex* which comes true. But the tragedy of Maya is different from that of Macbeth or Oedipus. Her tragedy stems from mental aloofness or psychic alienation while Macbeth's tragedy has its germs in his own folly, his overambitiousness. As to the tragedy of Oedipus, it can be said that he is no more than a chattel in the hands of God. Placed in the position of Oedipus, Maya would not have gathered the temerity to challenge the astrologer's prediction that after four years of marriage one of the couple would die. To this prediction she sharply reacts, 'I will never marry!' The Greek view of life would not have allowed her to say so. If Sophocles would have written *Cry, the Peacock*, Maya would have listened to the prophecy of the astrologer silently and succumbed to it without comment whatsoever. But in that case, Maya would have been a mere passive agent, an automaton, an instrument in the hands of God. It would not have had the touch of modernity which makes it so interesting in its own way.

Anita Desai's two novels *Cry, the Peacock* and *Where Shall We Go This Summer?* have more than entertainment value. They make us think, they make us realize the stark truth. For the first time in Indian English fiction, the problem of conjugal rift, matrimonial acrimony and psychic alienation which is related to physical and sexual alienation have been discussed at such great length and with fineness and perfection of art. The problem of Sita, the heroine of Desai's novel, *Where Shall We Go This Summer?* is no different from that of Maya because both of them suffer the same sense of isolation and psychic alienation. Both Maya and Sita remain no more than shambled and smothered in spirit.

In *Where Shall We Go This Summer?* Anita Desai's stance against negative vision is obvious. The ideas that life is to be lived in spite of all nastiness, madness and tedium and boredom is effectively conveyed through Sita, a mother of four children who escapes the dull, unhappy and frantic existence to keep the child unborn, feels free for the first time on the Manori island. She gains the painful awareness that life must be 'continued and all its business.' (167) There is courage in escaping from life and the city and in refusing 'to give birth to a child in a world not fit to receive the child.' (230) In portraying Sita who is opposed to urban society and forces of life accepts life as it is and by stressing her inner conflicts, Anita Desai gives the impression that life, in spite of the contraries that assail it, has to be lived because 'the existent life in constant interaction with other existences or existence is being with others.' Usha Bande analyzes Anita Desai's novels—*Cry, the Peacock* and *Where Shall We Go This Summer?* in the light of psychology and throws sufficient light on some unlit corners of Desai's fiction and shows how these novels are an attempt to locate and forge a meaningful pattern in an apparently chaotic world of despair and alienation.

Arun Joshi gives a congruent fictive form to still another dimension of incommunication. His protagonists Sindi Oberoi, Billy Biswas and Som Bhaskar are variations of the same anti-hero embodying chaos and uncertainty, torn by doubts, walking tight-rope between life and death, body and spirit, illusion and reality. His first novel *The Foreigner* incorporates both existentialism and the concept of detachment preached in the *Gita*. Sindi's dilemma is different from that of Srinivas in *The Nowhere Man* and Maya in *Cry, the Peacock*. Denied love, familial nourishment and cultural roots, he becomes a wandering alien like Naipaul's 'Unanchored Soul' or Camus' 'Outsider.' Sindi Oberoi wanders through the maze of existence but he is not able to find any purpose of life till he comes to India by chance, and when he visits Mr. Khemka, he is struck by the bronze figure of dancing Shiva. He is held, as it were in supreme ecstasy, "For a moment, just one brief moment, I was struck by the intense beauty of the divine dancer. America, India, Egypt, all mingled behind him in icons of increasing rhythm." (230) Soon after, he offers to do a meaningful job. Gradually he begins to feel sympathy for the labourers working for Mr. Khemka. His preoccupation with self crumbles and he is further and further drawn towards sympathetic attachment with the life of others. He takes over the management of imprisoned Mr. Khemka's business. The change of Mr. Sindi Oberoi has not been gladly accepted by some critics and they are of the opinion that the sudden acceptance is forced and therefore an artistic failure. This may not be agreed to. The novelist seems to have "felt the teahings of the *Gita* in his pulses and in this novel he has worked out the allegory of a benighted soul finding its salvation." (37) In fact, the novel ends on a suggestive note: from Boston to Delhi, Sindi Oberoi makes a journey: "from alienation to arrival, from selfishness to sacrifice, from an anomic responsible to himself, to a member of mankind, from being to becoming." (193)

The Last Labyrinth makes the search for anchorage in life, deeper and more powerful. Bhaskar's dilemma is the cry of a soul in agony who wants to know what is reality:

> Anuradha, listen. Listen to me wherever you are. Is there a God where you are? Have you met Him? Does He have a face? Does He speak? Does He hear? Does he understand the language that we speak. Anuradha, if there is a God tell Him I am weary. Of so many fears; so much doubting. Of this dark earth and these empty heavens. (166)

He is a quest hero craving for faith and meaning, "I want to know, probably I want to believe. But one can't order belief." (230) Som is like a bird that flutters its wings inside the cage and tries to get out of it but is helpless to do so. The personality of Som Bhaskar is enigmatic and it is difficult to understand his character in precise terms. All through the novel, he remains illusive. The labyrinth metaphor suggests the blind alley leading to death. Som Bhaskar is fully aware of his situation, his predicament, the impending danger which lurks behind his adventure, but he pretends to know nothing. He is a prey to self-deception. He exists and exists not. This polarity is presented by the novelist in such a telling manner that the dilemma of modern existence comes before us in all its ugliness and perversity. But Som who initially is lost in the labyrinth of life and death gradually gains understanding and moves towards realization. "We are all children trying to reach up to a crack in the door to peep into a room."[1]

Eliot illustrates the basic truth of enduring literature when he remarks that art must present, "beneath beauty and ugliness the boredom and the horror" as well as "the glory of life."[2] These contemporary novels do not merely crystallize the sociological, psychological and metaphysical facets of alienation into a poignant vision of life but also vindicate the novelists' deep concern for the story of life. Literature is not a political platform. Literature suggests, deepens and intensifies human response. These novels do touch the inner cords of readers and render them more human and illumined through suffering, understanding and courage.

The future of Indian English fiction is bright. It is moving in all the directions horizontally, diagonally and spirally, embracing all the possible facets of modern life. This diversification has proved fruitful because it has enabled the Indian English novelists to touch upon all the growing problems of modern complex life. The dynamism with which the Indian English novelists are facing these problems and the language and style which they have wielded to give voice to their experiences well suit the changed circumstances and the new world we live in. The idiom which Kamala Markandaya, Anita Desai and Arun Joshi use is not the idiom used by their predecessors. It is refreshing and it has a flexibility of its own.

Alienation whether it is cultural, psychic or existential is always painful. The question whether this alienation will persist or will be resolved through reconciliation, or understanding deserves serious consideration. There are clear inklings in the novels of Kamala Markandaya, Anita Desai and Arun Joshi that sooner or later this alienation will turn into arrival, the tangle will be solved, the tension will be mitigated and harmony and equipoise will prevail at last.

The ultimate message implicit in Kamala Markandaya's novels *The Coffer Dams* and *The Nowhere Man* are reconciliation and rapprochement. The heroine of Anita Desai's *Where Shall We Go This Summer?* at last finds a way through her much disturbed life and finally settles down with her husband in Bombay. Arun Joshi also believes in the ultimate goodness of man. All through Arun Joshi's novel *The Last Labyrinth* Anuradha remains an illusion. It is difficult to believe that she can love any young man faithfully and truly. But as the story proceeds we are face to face with her qualities as a beloved who can make monumental sacrifices for her lover. If she surreptitiously escapes from Lal Haveli, she does so only to save the life of Som Bhaskar. Som Bhaskar is something like a moth coming nearer everyday to the flame. Anuradha has the rare quality of self-abnegation which can immortalize any beloved.

Kiran Desai's first novel *Hullabaloo in the Guava Orchard* and her second novel *The Inheritance of Loss* are of great topical interest. Though the tone of her first novel does not accord with the tone of her second novel, the theme of alienation is her main concern in the second novel, *The Inheritance of Loss*. The seeds of alienation may be found intertwined in the structural design of her first novel in as much as it highlights the exploration of identity in a superstition-stricken world. The dialectics of blind faith and emancipation from fanaticism and fake religiosity versus logical reasoning is probed through a satirical story which is highly vivifying, titillating and sense-provoking. Sampat Chawla's every bit of gesture provokes peals of laughter. In *The Inheritance of Loss*, Kiran Desai dilates anguish of a westernized Indian, Jemubhai Popat Lal Patel, who is an ICS Officer and when he comes back to India from England, he is in a fix to decide who he is. He is neither an English man nor an Indian. He struggles for his identity. He feels utterly alienated in his own motherland. Kiran Desai with fine artistic strokes describes his aloofness, his loneliness, his dilemma.

It is heartening to note that these novelists believe in the theory of reconciliation and revival. The tie of understanding will hold fast. Acrimony, misunderstanding, loss of faith will be gone. Alienation will take the shape of arrival. Disillusionment if any will be dispelled. Cultural alienation will be replaced by world culture and world citizenship. Love, trust and confidence will tone down psychic alienation in conjugal life. Self-assertion will fight out the problem of existential alienation. After all Aurobindo's concept of the dawning of the Super Mind on earth is not a myth. Let us hope that the future will be brighter than the present. It is dubious to hold that there is evil in good. It is always wise to distinguish between real good from real evil. An optimist always does so. It is always an iconoclast and pessimist who is obsessed with the idea of gloomy future. Let future bring us hope, reconciliation and alleviation.

NOTES

1. *Existentialism and Alienation in American Literature* (International Publishers, New York), p. 13.
2. *The Sane Society* (Rinehart, New York, 1955), p. 122.

Chetan Bhagat's *One Night @ the Call Centre*: A Probe into the Present-Day Dynamics of Male-Female Relationship

Written "at the most conscious point of the race,"[1] to use a phrase of F.R. Leavis, Chetan Bhagat's recent novel, *One Night @ the Call Centre*, presents a horrifying picture of the fast changing facets of social scenario, particularly, with regard to the present-day dynamics of male-female relationship, in which the characters are all engaged in some kind of adventure knowing little or nothing of their surroundings. Larded with scientific jargons and technical keywords like website, computer, Italian bistro, strategic variables, Brad Pitt etc., the novel gives an impression of the author's flair for inventing a new idiom for fictional narrative that can keep pace with contemporary sensibility.

One Night @ the Call Centre is Chetan's second novel, his first novel being *Five Point Someone* (2004). Both the novels inspired Bollywood films. Amusement, which is one of the important ingredients of a good novel, is abundantly found in *One Night @ the Call Centre*. But it has something more. It is an in-depth study of male-female psyche which is given the form of an interesting story. It touches the delicate chord of the heart of the young generation because it voices its vibrations. Its story sounds less a story and more a sordid reality.

The novel has a dramatic opening. On an overnight train journey in the winter of 2004, from Kanpur to Delhi, the novelist comes across a young girl. The novelist steals time to ask her to tell a story to mitigate fatigue of the journey and to make it a pleasant one and the latter accedes to his proposal provided her story is given a book form. The novelist, in the beginning slightly hesitates, but later accepts the condition and the outcome is the present novel. The story is all about love and marriage. The characters portrayed are lively, good tempered, adventurous, free mixing, talkative, amiable, open-hearted. They pronounce each word with American accent.

The novelist does not crowd the novel with a galaxy of characters as Dickens often does, but in the manner of Zola and Turgenev, concentrates on a few characters focusing on their tastes, ambitions, and aptitudes. In the Prologue itself, the novelist makes it clear that it is a story "about six people, three guys and three girls who work at the Connections call centre. I chose to tell the story through Shyam's eyes. This is because after I met him I found him the most similar in me as a person. The rest of the people and what happened that night—well I will let Shyam tell you that." (13) The team of six people who work at the call centre in Gurgaon constitutes of "Military uncle, Radhika, Esha, Vroom, Priyanka and me." (19) Vroom is the short form of Varun Malhotra, Shyam is Shyam Mehra, Radhika is Radhika Jha, Esha is Esha Singh, and 'Me' stands for Shyam. Shyam's call name is Sam Marcey, Vroom's call name is Victor Mell, Radhika's call name is Regina Jones and Esha's call name is Eliza Singer.

Apart from these characters, there are a few subsidiary characters like Shefali, Ganesh Gupta, Anuj, Subhash Bakshi and Payal. Bakshi is the boss and over all in-charge of the call centre. His is a very deceptive personality. At the end of the novel, he emerges as a moral decrepit asking "girls for sexual favours in exchange for job." (235) The girls raise a voice of protest against him. Vroom insists on his tendering resignation: "So you will do the resignation letter, okay." (239) All these people assemble at the call centre at night and therefore the abbreviation ONCC is very suggestive.

The principal character of the novel is Shyam, a replica of the novelist. He is in love with Priyanka, the heroine of the novel. His past dates with Priyanka are described in five successive chapters, each revelatory of the curves of her delicate relationship with Priyanka. His fluctuating romance, his lewdity, his confusion, his conflict, his frailty, Priyanka's changing mood, her attraction and detraction, the ups and downs of her determination are all crystallized with a few surrealistic touches. Her love is treated on wholly practical, rather physical basis wiping out the distinction between love and lust.

In modern times, love is mostly fleshly and fornication, that is to say, voluntary sexual intercourse between persons not married to each other is a frequent sight. But both the sexes have to reap the bad consequences that follow in its train. The jerks and jolts they feel some times become irredeemable. In the beginning Shyam's love for Priyanka is purely aesthetic. When Priyanka asks him as to what makes him love her, he grows lyrical and in one single breath replies: "I love the kohl in your eyes, I love it when your eyes light up when you have gossip for me. I love it that you say you don't want desert and then ask me to change mine so you can have half. I love your stories about your mother. I love that you believe in me and are patient with my career. Actually, you know what, Priyanka? . . . I may not be a heart surgeon—but the one little heart I have, I have given it to you." (88-89) Ostensibly, there is no smell of sexual lust in the emotional outpouring of Shyam and it does not smack of cheapness either. But who knows when and how man changes and from a God he is transformed into a veritable beast. Freud is not wrong when he says that sex is the greatest drive of life. Slowly and gradually Shyam treads an untrodden path. After a month or so, he meets Priyanka. He makes advances in his love and something happens which is not unexpected. Priyanka sits in the lap of Shyam with one leg on each side. He puts a question to Priyanka: "are you crazy or are you drunk?" (103) The romantic reverie leads them to be lost in dreamy and pleasant thoughts.

> She unbuttoned the top few buttons of my shirt. Both. "Okay mister, the thing about confined spaces is that you have to cooperate. Now move your hands out of way," she said.
>
> We were quiet apart from our breathing. She confirmed that the windows were shut and ordered me to remove my shirt. She took off her kurti first, and then slowly unhooked her bra.
>
> "Be careful with your clothes. We'll need to find them quickly afterwards," she said "Are you mad. . . ." I gasped even as I raised my arms so she could pull my shirt over my head. She moved to keep my shirt aside and her foot landed on my left baby toe.
>
> "Ouch!," I screamed.

> "Oops, sorry," she said in a naughty apologetic tone. As she moved her foot away, her head hit the roof.
>
> "It's alright, clumsy sex is better than choreographed sex. And certainly better than no sex," I said as I pulled her close.
>
> We laughed as she embraced me. She started kissing me on my face. I kissed her shoulders.
>
> Twenty minutes later, we collapsed in each other's arms on the back seat. (103-4)

The description reads like a page from Alberto Moravia's *The Woman of Rome* or D.H. Lawrence's *Lady Chatterley's Lover*. But it should be borne in mind that the novelist sets out not to bring in Gods and Goddesses in his novel but to find normal human beings with all their weaknesses and shortcomings particularly in the modern context. Such steps and hazards as are taken by Shyam and Priyanka often lead to frustration and take much time in healing the wound. But who can deny that this aberration is permeated in the blood of the younger generation which it can hardly get rid of?

Shyam is against settled marriage. He is allergic to 'arrange marriage' because in an arranged marriage the parents trade their daughters to the highest bidder caring little for love or feelings. "Show me the money and keep our daughter for the rest of your life! That is the arrangement in an arranged marriage." (106)

The love between Shyam and Priyanka does not endure. It breaks with a sharp crack. Priyanka's mother does not like to give her daughter's hand to a man who is not properly settled in life. She is on the look out for a husband for Priyanka who is financially well off and can afford to make her daughter happy in every way. When Shyam and Priyanka meet next time, they feel the distance. Priyanka's mother settles the marriage of Priyanka with one Ganesh Gupta, Mr. Microsoft NRI, earning a lot in America and is coming to India next month. Priyanka is to get married the very next month. Shyam is flabbergasted to hear this news. He thrusts the responsibility of the malady on Priyanka's mother who, as he thinks, is a psychological case, "your mom is a psycho." (139) The lover and the beloved blame each other on this or that count. Shyam asks Priyanka as to what her mother wants and what she wants. Priyanka gives a categorical answer: "She wants me to show that I love her. She wants me to make her happy and marry someone she chooses for me." (139) "She is my mother. It is not as if she does not know what is good for me. I want someone doing well in his career as well." (140) Shyam's reaction is: "You used to eat at truck driver's dhabhas. Now all of a sudden you need an N.R.I Cardiac Surgeon to make ends meet?" (141) Their love relationship is snapped "A kiss was out of question." (141)

The bitterness in the relationship between Shyam and Priyanka comes to its climax when they meet next at Pizza Hut, Sahara Mall, Gurgaon, four months before this night. "They are meeting to formerly breakup." (171)

They work together at the call centre and as Priyanka says, "if there is tension between us, it will make it difficult to focus on work—for us and for others." (172) Priyanka is wedded to Ganesh Gupta and now she becomes Priyanka Gupta. Priyanka tells Shyam, "we can still be friends." (172) Ganesh offers a costly dark blue Indica Lexus to Priyanka on the eve of marriage and takes her to a five star hotel. Meanwhile Shyam and Priyanka receive a phone call from God. In fact, it is their conscience that speaks. Addressing Shyam, God says, "There are four things a person needs for success . . . one, a medium account of intelligence, and two, a bit of imagination, the third is what Shyam has lost self-confidence . . . the fourth ingredient is the most painful one . . . failure . . . to be really successful, you must face failure. You have to experience it, feel it, and suffer it. Only then you can shine." (221)

With the passage of time, Priyanka realises that she is in possession of every comfort of life, but has missed real love. She once again turns to Shyam. But Shyam neither wants to become a "sparewheel" (263) nor is happy over Priyanka's "sympathy decision." (261) Priyanka is in quest of real love which is denied to her. She gets a husband but loses her love. Priyanka, after a good deal of consideration, decides to marry Shyam, "I want to marry you Shyam." She admits: "I love you. Because you are the only person in the world I can be myself with." (261) In a penitent and remorseful tone, she says: "Hell, I prefer truck driver dhabhas over five-star hotels." (262)

Thereafter the lover and the beloved meet each other after six months. This big gap brings them nearer to each other. They are finally reconciled. An understanding is created between them. Shyam gets what he has lost. "All I could see was Priyanka, and all I could hear was my inner voice that said—Kiss her, kiss her and kiss her once more." (263)

Priyanka works at Connexions as before. But in six months, she is scheduled to take admission in a college for one-year B.Ed. course. Shyam's last impression is, " (i) I can do whatever I really want. (ii) God is always with me and (iii) there is no such thing as loser after all." (271)

The love-affair between Radhika and Anuj and Esha and Vroom forms an integral part of the main story. Radhika is a fickle-minded girl. She is more than romantic. Now she is married to Anuj. She is the only married one in the team. She wants to become a model. She aspires to be called Miss Universe. Her ambition is to hoard money, have a harmonious conjugal life and to make her mother-in-law happy. Radhika doubts whether her love for her husband is properly received by him. Vroom plays a radio jockey. He says that he would call Anuj and pretend that he is being called from a radio show. He would tell him that "he has won a prize, a large bouquet of roses and a box of Swiss chocolates that he can send to anyone he loves, any one in India with a loving message. So then we all get to hear what romantic lines he says to you." (156) The gimmick, however, does not succeed. Anuj calls from Kolkata that he would like to send the message to his girlfriend Payal who lives in Delhi and is a "modern type of girl." (157) Radhika is taken aback to know that the man on whom she reposed her faith has betrayed her and is looking for another girl, "Payal? What did you just say, Anuj? Your girlfriend Payal?" (157)

For the first time, she curses her husband since she got married. She takes headache pills. A chain of circumstances compels Radhika to think of severing her relationship with Anuj. With the help of Military Uncle, she finds a tough divorce lawyer. She says: "I am in no mood to compromise." (257) She lives marooned from all human relationships. Such is precisely the predicament of every modern girl who cares little for domesticity and more for self-aggrandizement. When a wife runs after the glitter and glamour of life and pays little heed to the requirements of her husband and refuses to retrace her steps to the noble ways of life in keeping with the tenets of pious existence, she is doomed to lose her husband who is likely to go astray and the marriage must end in nullity. This also accounts for the suffering of Grace Malbury in Hardy's *Woodlanders* and the frustration of Suman in Munshi Premchand's *Sevasadan*. Military Uncle is a dotard. Family feud makes him cut off from the members of his family. He lives all alone in the evening of his life. But the memory of his grandson rends his heart.

The fate of Esha is somewhat different from that of Radhika. She loves Shyam's friend Vroom. Esha is also Vroom's obsession. He thinks about Esha day and night. Vroom says to Esha, "I have been thinking about you a lot lately." (127) Esha interrogates, "Really?" (127) She looks sideways to ensure that Shyam is not eavesdropping the conversation which passes on between her and Vroom. But she knows that Vroom has no steady track of mind. He is like a butterfly roaming from flower to flower. Vroom had no hesitation in admitting it. "Yes really, Esha, I may have met a lot of girls, but no one is like you." (128) Esha giggles and takes a flower out from the vase and starts plucking out its petals.

Vroom is a professed lover. He pretends to love Esha and Esha well knows that behind the artificial gesture of Vroom there are hidden treachery, duplicity and double-dealing. Vroom tells Esha, "I think rather than fool around; I could do with a real relationship. So, I am asking you again—will you go out with me?" (128) Esha's reply is, "I don't know. How about a yes?" (128) Vroom does not understand as to why Esha is not interested in his proposal. But in no time, he understands, "if a girl hints she is not interested it's time to cut losses and quit. Never try the persuasion game." (128) There is reasonable cause why Esha is not interested in Vroom. Many a time, she tells Vroom that she wants to adopt the career of a model. Addressing Vroom, she says, "I've told you before. I have to focus on my modeling career. I can't afford the luxury of making a boyfriend." (36)

If Esha rejects Vroom, there is plausible cause behind it. The cause is that Vroom is a veritable philanderer who is in the habit of making love without serious intentions. Esha knows it, "that's right, with three different girlfriends last year, I am sure you will always be there for me." (128) Vroom takes a plea, the other girls were just for movie or something. They are channel surfing, you are more serious." (128)

Esha amazingly asks, "So what serious channel am I? The BBC?" (128) Vroom's statement borders on obscenity that amounts to social obloquy. "I have known you for more than a year. We have spent hundreds of nights together." (129) Saying so, Vroom extends his hands to hold the hands of Esha. Esha smells the foul play of Vroom and pulls her hands away nanoseconds before he reached it." (41) She gets agitated and her anger is flared up and she tells Vroom: "please stop it." (129) Vroom talks to Esha, as it were, she is a harlot. Esha cannot tolerate it. It is no romance but stupidity. Esha is no desperate nymphomaniac, like Lady Brett in Hemingway's *The Sun Also Rises* who loves Jake and finding him physically incapable of making love, is obliged, in order to satisfy her imperious needs, to take for lover now one, now another. Esha is not an unchaste girl and she cannot put up with an ever-changing lover like Vroom. Vroom does not feel comfortable at the call centre. But he gets on to show off his personality. He looks down upon his American employers.

The persons and all the girls who are attached to the call centre are loving, mentally alert, amiable, good-tempered, lively and high-spirited. The call centre abounds in pleasant personalities who enjoy talking to each other, sharing their feelings and ambitions.

With meticulous attention to securing the right word in the right place, Chetan develops a brilliant prose style, simple and direct. His mastery of language, his range of vocabulary, his power to create words and phrases and to use them to render the impact of sensation on the nerves and above all, his unique virtuosity, are everywhere manifested. Through words with their complex multiple associations, the novelist attempts to communicate a sense of simultaneity. He summons all meaning to judgment before a verbal apocalypse.

After graduating from I.I.T., Delhi, in 1995 and obtaining an M.B.A degree from I.I.M., Ahmedabad, Chetan Bhagat has picked up a job with an American investment bank. He is a creative genius and by writing novels on topical interest, has made a mark on contemporary Indian English literature.

NOTES

1. F.R. Leavis, *New Bearings in English Poetry* (London, 1932).
2. Chetan Bhagat, *One Night @ the Call Centre* (Delhi: Rupa, 2008).

Aravind Adiga's *The White Tiger*: An Anatomy of Deepening Moral Crisis in New India

The recent award of Man Booker Award (£ 50,000) for Aravinda Adiga's novel *The White Tiger* (2008) aroused surprise and curiosity among many a novel-loving reader. A question was put: "what is special in this novel which merits this much-coveted award?" Adiga is 37 (born 1974) and this novel is his maiden attempt.

Portillo, the chief, had high opinion about *The White Tiger*. He praised it in high-flown words: "Adiga undertakes an extraordinary task as he gains and holds key attention of the reader for a hero who is a thorough going villain." He also praised the author's attention to important social issues: the division between rich and poor and issues on a global scale. And it is extremely readable. Portillo's remark was: "The feeling among the readers was that here was a book on the cutting edge, reading with a different aspect of India, unfamiliar perhaps to many readers. What set it apart was its originality. The feeling was that this was a new territory." Portillo also likened the novel to Shakespeare's tragic play *Macbeth* which deals with an "ambition realized through murder." But the novelist here gave it a "delicious twist." Whereas Lady Macbeth and Macbeth are driven mad by their crime, the hero of this book is only driven mad by the fact that he hesitates and might not have committed murder.

The White Tiger, the much-talked of novel, is about economic disparity so conspicuous in modern Indian society. It tells the pathetic tale of two eras, one that still clings to the old decaying moral values and another that is anxious to accept the fast-emerging new moral values. Its anti-hero is Balram who is a complex character. He is the son of an impoverished rickshaw puller, Vikram Halwai. He is a servant, a car driver, an entrepreneur and a murderer rolled into one. He himself tells how the symbolic name "White Tiger" was given to him. Balram received his primary education in the village school where the Inspector once came on a surprise visit and put a question to him. The incident is narrated as follows:

> The inspector pointed his case straight at me, 'you, youngman, are an intelligent, honest, vivacious fellow in this crowd of thugs and idiots. In any jungle, what is the rarest of animals—the creature that comes along only once in a generation?'
>
> I thought about it and said: 'The White Tiger.'
>
> 'That what you are, in this jungle'
>
> Before he left, the inspector said, 'I'll write to Patna asking them to send you scholarship. You need to go to a real school. Somewhere far away from here. You need a real uniform, and a real education.'
>
> He had a parting gift for me—a book. I remember the title very well: *Lessons for the young boys from the life of Mahatma Gandhi*. So, that's how I became the White Tiger. (1)

This is how Balram came to be known as "White Tiger." He is indeed a rare distinct commodity from others on account of his special endowments of head and heart, and can be singled out for his outspokenness.

Balram like a typical Shavian protagonist is the mouthpiece of the novelist. Whatever the novelist has to say, he puts it in the mouth of Balram. The novel is shaped in the form of seven letters addressed by Balram to the Chinese premier on the eve of state visits. The story of the novel ranges over a period of five nights and four mornings. As the story proceeds, the force of the narrator grows more and more ironic, pungent and sardonic. In the later part of the story, a dismal and sombre atmosphere pervades and the novelist is in a fix to decide what is good and what is bad. The socio-economic crisis is expressed through characters and chain of incidents. Balram is the resident of village Laxmangarh in the district of Gaya. The story of the novel shifts from the Laxmangarh to Dhanbad, Bodh Gaya and then to Delhi and finally to Bangalore. The novelist adopts an epistolary method to describe his story. He writes to Ven Jiabao, the Chinese Premier, in order to apprise him of the changing facts of India. Even if the novelist had not referred to the name of the Chinese Premier, it would have made no difference and he would have conveniently described his story independently in the form of a report. However by adopting the technique of fictional narrative, the novelist gives an added charm to his account. The novel evinces maturity in handling a thought-provoking theme. It is wrapped in a language quite suited to the subject. It is fraught with antithetical expressions, scintillating with sarcasm. The novelist in a relentless style and with the help of pithy phrases exposes the hollowness discernible on multiple levels of modern society and ruthlessly attacks the so-called ideal marriage institution, electoral system, Parliamentary democracy, and modernization of big cities. He, without fear or frown, presents satirical portraits of the rich, the bigwigs, the politicians, the educationists, the doctors, the social reformers and the elites engaged in different vocations. Not that the novelist is not conscious of India's glorious past. But apparent from every part of his description is that he is highly sceptical of the new awakening that has taken place in India after independence. His scathing criticism over the post-Independence scenario is put in the mouth of Balram as follows:

> See, this country, in the days of greatness, when it was the richest nation on earth, was like a zoo. A clean well-kept, orderly zoo. Everyone in his place, everyone happy. Goldsmiths here, cowherds here, landlords here. The man called a Halwai sold sweets. The man called a cowherd tended cows. The untouchable cleaned dirt and filth. Landlords were kind to their servants. Women covered their heads with a veil and turned their eyes to the ground when talking to strange men. And then thanks to all those politicians in Delhi, on the fifteenth of August, 1947, the day the British left, the cages had been left open, and the animals had attacked and ripped each other apart and jungle law replaced zoo law. (63-64)

The inkling is that as soon as India attained independence, the politicians ran amuck with lustful eyes to grab the chair and they became worse than animals in their greed. Balram says: "Let animals live like animals; let humans live like humans. That's my whole philosophy in a sentence." (276)

There was a time when there were numerous castes in India. The number of castes went on multiplying with the passage of time. But the position is now different. No one cares for caste. The discrimination on the basis of caste is disappearing. Now there are only two castes in India, the rich and the poor. "To sum up—in the old days, there were one thousand castes and destinies in India. These days there are just two castes: Men with Big Bellies and Men with Small Bellies. And only two destinies: eat—or get eaten up." (64)

Balram's father is a patient of consumption. There is no hospital in Laxmangarh. Balram mocks at the duplicity of the politicians who show great gestures before election and after they win the race, they turn a deaf ear to the public interest. Balram says: "The hospital could not be constructed although there are three foundation stones laid by three different politicians before three different elections." (47)

The position of government hospital is all the more deplorable. There is one Lohia Universal Free Hospital founded by the great socialist leader Dr. Rammanohar Lohia. Balram's father is spitting blood. Balram, with the help of his brother Kishan, takes his father to the government hospital. But to his utter amazement, there is no doctor available there. He is told that some Dr. Ram Pandey is on duty. The ward boy, after he is bribed rupees ten, discloses that the said doctor may come in the evening. Other patients suffering from this or other diseases keep waiting. It is a bitter experience; the novelist through a Muslim character describes the rot in the procedure of appointment of doctors in government hospitals. The medical superintendent is entrusted with the task to supervise the working of junior doctors. Whenever the place of a doctor falls vacant, the Great socialist lets all the big doctors know that the post will be filled by auction and the rate for the post is around four hundred thousand rupees. The job is given to the highest bidder. When appointed, the newly appointed doctor passes on one third of his salary to the medical superintendent and lets the newcomer work in private hospitals caring little for the village government hospitals and submits perfunctory report of his regular presence by making a tick in the ledger. This is how government hospitals run on paper. The rot is not on one level but on various levels. And the pity is that we crow on the dunghill of rejections.

After the death of his father, Balram comes to Dhanbad along with his brother Kishan and his cousin Dilip and picks up the humble job of a servant in a tea shop. He describes that the servants in tea shops are "human spiders that go crawling in between and under the tables with rags in their hands, crushed humans in crushed uniforms, sluggish, unshaven in their thirties or forties but still boys." (51) Balram admits that he works "with near total dishonesty, lack of dedication and insincerity." (51)

Balram is highly susceptible by nature. The present social set up in India is a puzzle to him. He says: "Never before in human history have so few owed so much to so many, Mr. Jiabao. A handful of men in this country have trained the remaining 99.9 percent—as strong, as talented, as intelligent in every way to exist in perhaps servitude; servitude so strong that you can put the key of his emancipation in a man's hand and he will throw it back at you with a curse." (175-76)

Balram is a simpleton. He is noted for his simplicity and credulity. He is neither a profound thinker nor a philosopher. He admits: "The story of his upbringing is the story of how a half baked fellow is produced." (11) But he is not sorry for it. He says: "We entrust our glorious parliamentary democracy . . . to characters like these." (10) Is his attack ill-directed? It is a matter of common experience that there is no dearth of members of parliament who are 'half-baked.'

The life of Balram turns a new leaf when he is appointed a chauffer by a landlord of Laxmangarh for his son, daughter-in-law and his two pomerian dog's cuddles and puddles. Mr. Ashok has two drivers Ram Prasad and Balram. Ashok is very fond of pomp and show and everything gorgeous. He resides in a lovely old mansion. He had wedded Pinky, a Christian, in America and now lived in India. He often plays badminton with his wife in the compound of his house. She wears trousers. Ashok was born in village Laxmangarh though he had never seen it. Balram first met Ashok at Dhanbad and later he was taken to Delhi. Balram continues his studies there. He wants to break the cage and unchain himself. The patronage of Mr. Ashok infuses new hope and courage in him. He thinks of the city. He is told that Delhi is a living paradise. But his dream is soon shattered. In new India, Delhi is not meant for peace, solace, good administration, mental equipoise, harmony and honesty. It is a veritable hell, the seat of corruption. In the beginning, Balram's master Ashok is corrupted. Then the infection passes to Balram. Balram says about Ashok: "He returned from America an innocent man, but life in Delhi corrupted him—and once the master of the Honda city becomes corrupted, how can the driver stay innocent?" (197)

Balram's own confession is: "The rest of today's narration will deal mainly with the sorrowful tale of how I was corrupted from a sweet, innocent village fool into a citified fellow full of debauchery, depravity and wickedness." (197) Balram is an eyewitness to what is going on in Delhi—the capital of glorious India.

Balram lets the Chinese Premier know that servitude, the condition of being forced to work for others and having no freedom can be easily seen in Delhi. In the words of Balram: "every day millions wake up at dawn—stand in dirty crowded buses—get off at their master's posh houses—and then clean the floors, wash the dishes, weed the garden, feed their children, press their feet—all for a pittance: I will never envy the rich of America or England, Mr. Jiabao: They have no servants there." (176)

And at the rush hour in Delhi, the scene of traffic jams is all the more horrible: "Rush hour in Delhi. Cars, scooters, motorbikes, auto rickshaws, black taxis, jostling for space on the road. The pollution is so bad that the men on the motorbikes and scooters have a handkerchief wrapped around their faces—each time you stop at a red light, you see a row of men with black glasses and masks on their faces as if the whole city was out on a bank heist that morning." (133)

As a driver, Balram exposes the stark reality: "Let a driver tell you the truth. And the truth is that Delhi is a crazy city." (118) And again: "See, the rich people live in big housing colonies like Defence Colony or Greater Kailash or Vasant Kunj, and inside their colonies the houses have numbers and letters, but this numbering and lettering follows no known system or logic." (118-19)

The fate of rickshaw-pullers is pitiable. "Now since I doubt that you have rickshaw-pullers in China or in any other civilized nation on earth, you will have to see it for yourself. Rickshaws are not allowed inside the posh parts of Delhi, where foreigners might see them and gape, insist on going to Old Delhi, or Nizamuddin—there you will see the road full of them—thin stick like men leaning forward from the seat of a bicycle, as they pedal along a carriage bearing a pyramid of middle-class flesh some fat man with his fat wife and all their shopping bags and groceries. (27) And the scene of the chicken market in old Delhi is no less heart-rending and disgusting: "Go to old Delhi, behind the Jama Masjid, and look at the way they keep chickens in the market. Hundreds of pale hens and brightly-coloured roosters, stuffed lightly into wire-mesh cages, packed as tightly as worms in a belly, pecking each other and shitting each other, jostling just for breathing space; the whole cage giving off a horrible stench—stench of terrified, feathered flesh. On the wooden desk above the coop sits a grinning young butcher, showing off the flesh and organs of a recently chopped up chicken, with oleaginous with a coating of dark blood." (173)

Delhi, the centre of glory is laughed at and ridiculed. The book sellers in Old Delhi sell books on various subjects including sexual pleasure. "You may have heard of this market, sir, it is one of the wonders of the world. Tens of thousands of dirty, rotting, blackened books on every subject—Technology, Medicine, Sexual pleasure, Philosophy, Education and Foreign countries—heaped upon the pavement from Delhi Gate onwards all the way until you get to the market in front of the Red Fort. Some books were in Urdu, the language of the Muslims—which is all just scratches and dots, as if some crow dipped its feet and pressed them to the page." (252-53)

Balram frankly admits that his master Ashok, who is his ideal and whose foot prints he followed, was also tempted to indulge in romance with another girl other than his legitimate wife. Once he does romance with Ms. Uma, he spent more and more time with her. (267) Balram also finds a fat man moving on to a hotel with a golden haired girl. 'Taking liquor was a sign of good sense.' (279)

The novelist goes on piling up such damaging and uncharitable remarks on the corruption prevailing in Delhi. He also gives a telling account of how killing of servants by their masters is a frequent sign in Delhi. Balram narrates one such incident. A moneyed man had employed a domestic servant to guard his infant son. The boy was kidnapped by the Naxals and then tortured and killed. The servant was innocent. But the employer got four of his hired gunmen to torture the servant who was shot through his head. (67) Tyranny of police, nasty and obnoxious games, sexual offence, crime in the car and underhand practice are common features in this capital city of India. People live in a state of perpetual tension. Confusion, terror, suspicion, atrocity, duplicity, bamboozling, various kinds of cruelties reign supreme there. Then what is there in Delhi to be proud of? Balram is unable to understand where does lie the prestige of Delhi and for what we should claim to be the citizen of civilized nation. Balram describes what happens to drivers in Delhi everyday. Soon after an accident takes place, the driver is held and forced to swear an affidavit confessing his guilt. He himself once did so. The witness to this attainment was his grandmother Kusum and the identifier was Chamandas Varma, Advocate, Delhi High Court. (168)

In Delhi, the magazine *Murder Weekly* is published by the government of India publishers and is sold for just four and a half rupees to make it accessible to the general public. The magazine contains sensational news about murder, rape and revenge and is sold like a hot-cake at a cheap rate. Balram is least interested in the sensational stories published in the magazine *Murder Weekly*. He comes over to Delhi to earn his living. He looks upon his master Ashok as his father and benefactor much in the same manner in which Hanuman did towards Ram. But he has high ambitions. He loves to jump higher and higher. The story of his progress from a humble naïve village lad to a man with tall ambitions is highly tantalizing. As Macbeth's ambition could not have been fulfilled without removing King Duncan from his way, so Balram's ambition could not have been fulfilled without removing his multimillionaire master Ashok. He was sharp waiting for the ripe time. And once he gets it. He is driving the car with his master. Ashok has to withdraw heavy amount from the banks. They move from bank to bank and the weight of the red bag carried by Ashok increases. The amount withdrawn from the banks is seven hundred thousand rupees. Balram thought: "It was enough for a house, a motor bike and a small shop. A new life." (281) Balram asks Ashok to step down the car on the pretext that there is something wrong with the tyre. Ashok smells some foul play. "He put a hand on the door and was about to step out, but some instinct of self-preservation still held him back." (283) Sometimes Balram thinks to kill his master. But the other moment, good thought dawns upon him. "I'm losing him, I thought and this forced me to do something. I knew I would hate myself for, even years later." I really didn't want to do this, I really didn't want him to think, even with two or three minutes he had left to live, that I was that kind of driver—the one that resorts to black-mailing his master—but he had left me no option." (283) Balram is in a state of conflict. On the one hand, he asks Ashok "trust me" and on the other stands for distrust. He turns disloyal towards him and acts deceitfully. He is at a loss to decide what to do. But after a good deal of pondering, he takes the decision. He has no way but to murder Ashok. This alone can fulfill his ambition. He rams the strong bottle of wine on the head of Ashok and smashes it. "The stunned body fell into the mud. A hissing sound came out of its lips, like wind escaping from a tyre." (285)

Now the question arises whether the action of Balram can be justified on the touchstone of morality. His position is different from that of Macbeth who murders his master Duncan or from Clytemnestra who murders her husband Agamemnon. Macbeth too hesitates before he embarks upon the heinous crime. But the seed of criminality lies dormant in his character and it spurts when the opportune time comes. The serpent of criminality lies in its coils and it raises its hood when it is provoked. After the crime is committed, Macbeth is full of repentance. He is even driven to madness. His wife Lady Macbeth, who is instrumental in the crime, suffers from a serious mental disease, somnambulism, meaning sleep walking. Balram on the other hand after he commits the crime is not filled with regret or sense of remorse for his wrong-doing. His position is different from Clytemnestra. Like Clytemnestra, he does not justify his action or his morality nor does attitude lift him from the level of a criminal. His attitude is amoral in the sense that it falls outside the domain of morality. Balram's journey is a psychic journey. He is far away from Laxmangarh, his native place. But the house is within his mind. Once in Delhi he passes through a butcher's quarter. He finds a large cart driven by a buffalo. Surprisingly enough, there was no human sitting on the cart with a whip. The cart was packed with dead buffaloes. The buffalo knew on its own where to go. The buffalo turned its face to him and in a voice just like his father's, declared: "Your brother Kishan was beaten to death. Happy?" (256)

"Your aunt Lutti was raped and then beaten to death. Happy? Your grandmother Kusum was kicked to death. Happy?" (256) It is the voice of an animal, a weird voice. But Balram distinctly hears it. In fact it is a terrible, frightening nightmarish dream. Nothing is outside. It is the projection of Balram's guilty mind and where he is responsible for destroying all the members of his family.

The novel is replete with ironic remarks put in the mouth of this or that character. A few examples:

> "It's a divorce—every rich man these days is divorcing his wife." (183)
> "I've never heard of a landlord who was vegetarian." (83)
> "The dreams of the rich and the dreams of the poor—they never overlap, do they?" (225)

A large part of the novel is devoted to highlight the changing face of Delhi, particularly Old Delhi. Balram sarcastically says: "Remember, Mr. Premier, that Delhi is the capital of not one but two countries—two Indias. The light and the darkness both flow into Delhi. Gurgaon, where Mr. Ashok lived is the biggest modern end of the city, and this place, old Delhi, is the other end. Full of things that the modern forgot all about—rickshaws, old stone buildings, and Muslims." (251) The two Indias, one modern and another bygone are juxtaposed. The readers have to decide which one should be preferred.

Adiga has to transmit impressions of reality, be it good, bad, indifferent, cruel, mean or contemptible. His aim is to portray with the inevitability of life itself, man's wretchedness and helplessness. He observed man and life closely especially man under adverse conditions, man in the grip of elemental fear. He observes the process of mental and moral decay in new India after Independence. He watches attempts at regeneration failed by inner weakness and betrayed by self-delusion. The novel helps to quicken new ideas about the fast decaying moral values of Indian people and hastens the destruction of old morality based on ideology.

The White Tiger presents a masterly study of social antagonism—two factions with different economic conditions, one superior, another horrible, neither desiring to understand the other and one of them in the wrong place. The story of the novel is replete with the rollicking saliva coupled with unalloyed humour. The total effect of the novel is one of bitter disillusionment with society. The novelist explores a vanishing India where there is complete want of understanding between the high and the low, the rich and the poor and the emotional life has been evoked.

Virtually the whole story is conveyed through the lips of Balram who is deeply interested in letting us know the truth about new India. This character is more vividly realized by the novelist than any other character. For much of the story Balram is himself an eyewitness. He arrests our attention throughout. Human relations in great variety are touched off in a firm, sensitive, penetrating style. There is something joyous in the spontaneous flow of impressions from the novelist's unjaded pen. The novelist's style is brilliantly original.

Balram's grotesque desire to achieve his end by murdering his master may be approximated only by appreciating a typical modern man subjected to perpetual suffering. Like Eliot's Prufrock, he symbolizes the change in sensibility.

The novel has a well-knit and close-packed plot. Here and there, there are twists and turns in stylistic devices which heighten the effect of the narrative. The language is spontaneous. By and large the novel is a monumental piece of art.

NOTES

1. Aravind Adiga, *The White Tiger* (Harper Collins India, 2008).

Select Bibliography

Achebe, Chinua. *Things Fall Apart*, Heinemann, London, 1958.

_____. *No Longer at Ease*, Heinemann, London.

_____. "The Black Writers' Burden," *Presence Africaine*, 59, 1966, pp. 131-39.

_____. "Named for Victoria, Queen of England," *New Letters*, XI, 1973.

Adiga, Aravind. *The White Tiger*, Harper Collins India, 2008

Bala, Suman and D.K. Pabby, ed. *The Fiction of Anita Desai,* 2 vols. New Delhi: Prestige, 2000.

Bande, Usha. *The Novels of Anita Desai*, Prestige, New Delhi, 1988.

Belliappa, Meena. *Anita Desai—A Study of Her Fiction*, Writers Workshop, Calcutta, 1971.

Bhagat, Chetan. *One Night @ the Call Centre.* Rupa, Delhi, 2008.

Bhatnagar, O.P. "Arun Joshi's *The Foreigner*: A Critique of East and-West." *The Journal of Indian Writing in English*, 1-2 July, 1973.

Dalmia, Yashodhara. "An Interview with Anita Desai." *The Times of India*, April 29, 1979.

Desai, Anita. *Cry, the Peacock*, Peter Owen, London, 1965

_____. *Where Shall We Go This Summer?*, Vikas, Delhi, 1978.

_____. *Voices in the City*, Peter Owen, London, 1963.

_____. *Bye-Bye Blackbird*, Hind Pocket Books, Delhi, 1971.

_____. *Fire on the Mountain*, Penguin, U.S.A., 1984.

_____. *Clear Light of Day*, Allied, New Delhi, 1980.

_____. *In Custody*, Penguin Books, England, 1985.

_____. *Baumgartner's Bombay*, Penguin, London, 1988.

Desai, Kiran., *Hullabaloo in the Guava orchard*, New Delhi: Viking Penguin India, 1988

_____. *The Inheritance of Loss*, Penguin, 2006.

Dhawan, R.K. *The Fictional World of Arun Joshi*, Classical, New Delhi, 1986.

_____. *Indian Women Novelists*, 18 vols. Prestige Books, New Delhi, 1991-1995.

Ellison, Ralph. *Invisible Man*, The New American Library, New York, 1960

Eliot, T.S. 'Matthew Arnold.' *The Use of Poetry and the Use of Criticism*, London, 1933.

Frank, Johnson. *Alienation, Concept, Term and Meaning*, New York and London, 1973.

Fromm, Erich. *Zen Buddhism and Psychoanalysis*, New York, 1970.

Geetha, P. "Kamala Markandaya: An Interpretation," *Commonwealth Quarterly*, Vol. 3, no. 9, December 1978.

Ghosh, Tapan K. *Arun Joshi's Fiction*. New Delhi: Prestige.

Guruprasad, Thakur. "And never the Twain Shall meet; Kamala Markandaya's *The Nowhere Man*," *Language Forum*, Vol. VII, Nos. 1-4, April 1981-March 1982.

Heinemann, F.H. *The Existentialism and the Modern Predicament*, Adom and Charles Black, London, 1983.

Iver, Robert M. Mac. *The Ramparts We Guard*, Macmillan, New York, 1950.

Iyengar, K.R. Srinivasa. *Indian Writing in English*, Asia, Bombay, 1973.

Jain Jasbir. *Indian English Novelists*. Sterling, New Delhi, 1982

Jaspers, Karl. *Man in the Modern Age*, Trans. Eden and Cedar Paul, New York, 1956.

Joseph, Margaret P. *Kamala Markandaya*, Arnold Heinemann, New Delhi, 1980.

Joshi, Arun. *The Foreigner*, Hind Pocket Books, Delhi, 1968.

_____. *The Last Labyrinth*, Orient Paperbacks, New Delhi, 1981

_____. *The Strange Case of Billy Biswas*, Orient Paperbacks, Delhi, 1971.

_____. *The Apprentice*, Orient Paperbacks, Delhi, 1974.

_____. *The City by the River*, Vision Books, New Delhi, 1990.

Kalinnikova, E.J. *Indian English Literature: A Survey*, Vimal, Ghaziabad, 1982.

Katamble, V.D." *The Coffer Dams*: An Apology for Techno-Industrialisation of Rural India," *Vortex* I, October 1979.

Kohli, Suresh. "The Fiction of Anita Desai," *The Statesman* (Sunday Magazine Section), 6 Nov. 1977.

Kumar, Shiv K. "Tradition and Change in the Novels of Kamala Markandaya," *Osmania Journal of English Studies*, VII, No. 1, 1969.

Maini, D.S. "The Achievement of Anita Desai," *Indo-English Literature*, ed. K.K. Sharma. Vimal, Ghaziabad, 1977.

Markandaya, Kamala. *The Coffer Dams*, Hind Pocket Books, Delhi, 1973

_____. *The Nowhere Man*, Orient Longman, Bombay, 1975

Mathur, O.P. "The Existential Note in Arun Joshi," *Commonwealth Quarterly*, Vol. 5, December 1980.

_____. "From Existentialism to Karmayoga: A Study of Arun Joshi's *The Foreigner*," *The Alien Voice*, ed. A.K. Srivastava, Print House, Lucknow, 1981.

Mukherjee, Meenakshi. *Twice-Born Fiction*, Arnold Heinemann, New Delhi, 1972.

Naik M.K. *Aspects of Indian Writing in English*, Macmillan, Madras, 1979.

_____. *A History of Indian English Novel*, Sahitya Akademi, New Delhi, 1982.

Nandakumar, Prema. "Indian Writing in English; Three Cheers," *Indian Literature*, 13, No. 4.

Narasimhan, Raji. 'Desai versus Desai: Norms of Appreciation,' *Indian Literature*, Nos. 3-4, July-December 1975.

Parameswaran, Uma. *A Study of Representative Indo-English Novelists*, Vikas, New Delhi, 1976.

_____. "Indian for the Western Readers: A Study of Kamala Markandaya's Novels," *Texas Quarterly*, Vol. X, No. 2, Summer 1968.

Prasad, H.M. "The Quintessence of Kamala Markandaya's Art," *Commonwealth Quarterly*, Vol. 3, No. 9, December 1978.

_____. *Response: Recent Revelations on Indian Fiction in English*. PBD, Bareilly, 1983.

_____. *Arun Joshi*, Arnold Heinemann, 1986.

Prasad, Madhusudan. *Anita Desai: The Novelist*, New Horizon, Allahabad, 1981

_____. *Indian English Novelists: An Anthology of Critical Essays*, Sterling, New Delhi, 1982.

_____. *Perspectives on Kamala Markandaya*, Vimal, Ghaziabad 1984.

Raizada, Harish. *The Lotus and the Rose: Indian Fiction in English (1850-1947)*, Aligarh Muslim University, Aligarh, 1978.

Ram, Atma. "Anita Desai's *Where Shall We Go This Summer?*" *World Literature Written in English*, Vol. XV, No. 2, November 1976.

_____. "An Interview with Anita Desai," *World Literature Written in English*, Vol. XVI, No. 1, April 1977.

_____. "Indian Slow to Recognise Talent in Their Midst," *The Tribune*, June 26, 1977.

_____. "Anita Desai," *Journal of Indian Writing in English*, Vol. 5, No. 2, July, 1977.

_____. "Anita Desai. Exploration of Inner Sensibility," *Perspective*, July 1978.

_____. "Anita Desai," *National Herald*, June 26, 1980.

Rao, B. Ram Chandra. *The Novels of Anita Desai*. Kalyani, Delhi, 1977.

Rao, Nirmala. "Indian Expatriate," *Journal of Commonwealth Literature*, Vol. X, No. 3, April 1976.

Rao, Vimala. "Anita Desai's *Where Shall We Go This Summer?* An Analysis," *Commonwealth Quarterly*, December 1978.

Sharma, K.K. *Indo-English Literature: A Collection of Critical Essays*, Vimal, Ghaziabad, 1977.

Sharma, R.S. *Anita Desai*, Arnold Heinemann, New Delhi, 1981.

Singh, R.S. "Aloneness Alone: Anita Desai and Arun Joshi," *Indian Novels in English*, Arnold, Heinemann, New Delhi, 1977.

Williams, H.M. *Indian Fiction, New Writers (1945-70), Indo-Anglian Literature, 1800-1970: A Survey*, Orient Longman, New Delhi, 1976.

Srivastava, A.K. *Alien Voice*, Print house, Lucknow, 1981.

Srivastava, R.K., ed. *Perspective on Anita Desai*, Vimal, Ghaziabad, 1983.

Verghese, C. Paul. *Essays on Indian Writing in English*, N.V. publications, Bombay, 1975.